Simple Suppers

Publisher & Creative Director: Nick Wells
Project Editor: Sarah Goulding
Designer: Mike Spender
With thanks to: Gina Steer

This is a **FLAME TREE** Book

FLAME TREE PUBLISHING
Crabtree Hall, Crabtree Lane
Fulham, London SW6 6TY
United Kingdom
www.flametreepublishing.com

Flame Tree is part of The Foundry Creative Media Company Limited

First published 2005

Copyright © 2005 Flame Tree Publishing

07 09 08
5 7 9 10 8 6 4

ISBN 1 84451 335 1

A copy of the CIP data for this book is available from the British Library.

Printed in China

Simple Suppers

Quick and Easy Recipes

**FLAME TREE
PUBLISHING**

Contents

Contents

Vegetarian   **208**

Contents

Dinner Parties & Entertaining 270

Puddings & Desserts **348**

Index 382

Hygiene in the Kitchen

It is well worth remembering that many foods can carry some form of bacteria. In most cases, the worst it will lead to is a bout of food poisoning or gastroenteritis, although for certain people this can be more serious. The risk can be reduced or eliminated by good food hygiene and proper cooking.

Do not buy food that is past its sell-by date and do not consume any food that is past its use-by date. When buying food, use your eyes and nose. If the food looks tired, limp or a bad colour or it has a rank, acrid or simply bad smell, do not buy or eat it under any circumstances.

Do take special care when preparing raw meat and fish. A separate chopping board should be used for each; wash the knife, board and the hands thoroughly before handling or preparing any other food.

Regularly clean, defrost and clear out the refrigerator or freezer – it is worth checking the packaging to see exactly how long each product is safe to freeze.

Avoid handling food if suffering from an upset stomach as bacteria can be passed through food preparation.

Dish cloths and tea towels must be washed and changed regularly. Ideally use disposable cloths which should be replaced on a daily basis. More durable cloths should be left to soak in bleach, then washed in the washing machine on a boil wash.

Keep the hands, cooking utensils and food preparation surfaces clean and do not allow pets to climb on to any work surfaces.

Buying

Avoid bulk buying where possible, especially fresh produce such as meat, poultry, fish, fruit and vegetables unless buying for the freezer. Fresh foods lose their nutritional value rapidly so buying a little at a time minimises loss of nutrients. It also eliminates a packed refrigerator which reduces the effectiveness of the refrigeration process.

When buying prepackaged goods such as cans or pots of cream and yogurts, check that the packaging is intact and not damaged or pierced at all. Cans should not be dented, pierced or rusty. Check the sell-by dates even for cans and packets of dry ingredients such as flour and rice. Store fresh foods in the

refrigerator as soon as possible – not in the car or the office.

When buying frozen foods, ensure that they are not heavily iced on the outside and the contents feel completely frozen. Ensure that the frozen foods have been stored in the cabinet at the correct storage level and the temperature is below 18°C/-0.4°F. Pack in cool bags to transport home and place in the freezer as soon as possible after purchase.

Preparation

Make sure that all work surfaces and utensils are clean and dry. Hygiene should be given priority at all times. Separate chopping boards should be used for raw and cooked meats, fish and vegetables. Currently, a variety of good-quality plastic boards come in various designs and colours. This makes differentiating easier and the plastic has the added hygienic advantage of being washable at high temperatures in the dishwasher. (NB: If using the board for fish, first wash in cold water, then in hot to prevent odour!) Also, remember that knives and utensils should always be thoroughly cleaned after use.

When cooking, be particularly careful to keep cooked and raw food separate to avoid any contamination. It is worth washing all fruits and vegetables regardless of whether they are going to be eaten raw or lightly cooked. This rule should apply even to prewashed herbs and salads.

Do not reheat food more than once. If using a microwave, always check that the food is piping hot all the way through. In theory, the food should reach 70°C/158°F and needs to be cooked at that temperature for at least three minutes to ensure that all bacteria are killed.

All poultry must be thoroughly thawed before using, including chicken and poussin. Remove the food to be thawed from the freezer and place in a shallow dish to contain the juices. Leave the food in the refrigerator until it is completely thawed. A 1.4 kg/3 lb whole chicken will take about 26–30 hours to thaw. To speed up the process immerse the chicken in cold water. However, make sure that the water is changed regularly. When the joints can move freely and no ice crystals remain in the cavity, the bird is completely thawed.

Once thawed, remove the wrapper and pat the chicken dry. Place the chicken in a shallow dish, cover lightly and store as close to the base of the refrigerator as possible. The chicken should be cooked as soon as possible.

Some foods can be cooked from frozen including many prepacked foods such as soups, sauces, casseroles and breads. Where applicable follow the manufacturers' instructions.

Vegetables and fruits can also be cooked from frozen, but meats and fish should be thawed first. The only time food can be refrozen is when the food has been thoroughly thawed then

cooked. Once the food has cooled then it can be frozen again. On such occasions the food can only be stored for one month.

All poultry and game (except for duck) must be cooked thoroughly. When cooked the juices will run clear from the thickest part of the bird – the best area to try is usually the thigh. Other meats, like minced meat and pork should be cooked right the way through. Fish should turn opaque, be firm in texture and break easily into large flakes.

When cooking leftovers, make sure they are reheated until piping hot and that any sauce or soup reaches boiling point first.

Storing, Refrigerating and Freezing

Meat, poultry, fish, seafood and dairy products should all be refrigerated. The temperature of the refrigerator should be between 1–5°C/34–41°F while the freezer temperature should not rise above -18°C/-0.4°F.

To ensure the optimum refrigerator and freezer temperature, avoid leaving the door open for a long time. Try not to overstock the refrigerator as this reduces the airflow inside and affects the effectiveness in cooling the food within.

When refrigerating cooked food, allow it to cool down quickly and completely before refrigerating. Hot food will raise the temperature of the refrigerator and possibly affect or spoil other food stored in it.

Food within the refrigerator and freezer should always be covered. Raw and cooked food should be stored in separate parts of the refrigerator. Cooked food should be kept on the top shelves of the refrigerator, while raw meat, poultry and

fish should be placed on bottom shelves to avoid drips and cross-contamination. It is recommended that eggs should be refrigerated in order to maintain their freshness and shelf life.

Take care that frozen foods are not stored in the freezer for too long. Blanched vegetables can be stored for one month; beef, lamb, poultry and pork for six months and unblanched vegetables and fruits in syrup for a year. Oily fish and sausages should be stored for three months. Dairy products can last four to six months while cakes and pastries should be kept in the freezer for three to six months.

High-Risk Foods

Certain foods may carry risks to people who are considered vulnerable such as the elderly, the ill, pregnant women, babies, young infants and those suffering from a recurring illness.

It is advisable to avoid those foods listed below which belong to a higher-risk category.

There is a slight chance that some eggs carry the bacteria salmonella. Cook the eggs until both the yolk and the white are firm to eliminate this risk. Pay particular attention to dishes and products in-corporating lightly cooked or raw eggs which should be eliminated from the diet. Sauces including Hollandaise, mayonnaise, mousses, soufflés and meringues all use raw or lightly cooked eggs, as do custard-based dishes, ice creams and sorbets. These are all considered high-risk foods to the vulnerable groups mentioned above.

Certain meats and poultry also carry the potential risk of salmonella and so should be cooked thoroughly until the juices run clear and there is no pinkness left. Unpasteurised products such as milk, cheese (especially soft cheese), pâté, meat (both raw and cooked) all have the potential risk of listeria and should be avoided.

When buying seafood, buy from a reputable source which has a high turnover to ensure fresh-ness. Fish should have bright clear eyes, shiny skin and bright pink or red gills. The fish should feel stiff to the touch, with a slight smell of sea air and iodine. The flesh of fish steaks and fillets should be translucent with no signs of discolouration.

Molluscs such as scallops, clams and mussels are sold fresh and are still alive. Avoid any that are open or do not close when tapped lightly. In the same way, univalves such as cockles or winkles should withdraw back into their shells when lightly prodded. When choosing cephalopods such as squid and octopus they should have a firm flesh and pleasant sea smell.

As with all fish, whether it is shellfish or seafish, care is required when freezing it. It is imperative to check whether the fish has been frozen before. If it has been frozen, then it should not be frozen again under any circumstances.

Herbs & Spices

The use of herbs and spices can make all the difference between a bland and a tasty dish. A variety of the most common herbs and spices, along with their uses, are listed below.

ALLSPICE The dark allspice berries come whole or ground and have a flavour similar to that of cinnamon, cloves and nutmeg.

BASIL Best fresh but also available in dried form, basil can be used raw or cooked and works particularly well in tomato-based and mediterranean dishes.

BAY LEAVES Are available in fresh or dried form as well as ground. They make up part of a bouquet garni and are particularly delicious when added to meat and poultry dishes, soups, stews, vegetable dishes and stuffing. They also impart a spicy flavour to milk puddings and egg custards.

BOUQUET GARNI is a bouquet of fresh herbs tied with a piece of string or in a small piece of muslin. It is used to flavour casseroles, stews and stocks or sauces. The herbs that are normally used are parsley, thyme, and bay leaves.

CAYENNE Cayenne is the powdered form of a red chilli pepper said to be native to Cayenne. It is similar in appearance to paprika and can be used sparingly to add a fiery kick to many dishes.

CARDAMOM Cardamom has a distinctive sweet rich taste and can be bought whole in the pod, in seed form or ground. This sweet aromatic spice is delicious in curries, rice, cakes and biscuits and is great served with rice pudding and fruit.

CHERVIL Reminiscent of parsley and available either in fresh or dried form, chervil has a faintly sweet spicy flavour and is particularly good in soups, cheese dishes, stews and with eggs.

CHILLI Available whole, fresh, dried and in powdered form, red chillies tend to be sweeter in taste than their green counterparts. They are particularly associated with Spanish and Mexican-style cooking and curries.

CHIVES This member of the onion family is ideal for use when a delicate onion flavour is required. Chives are good with eggs, cheese, fish and vegetable dishes. They also work well as a garnish for soups, meat and vegetable dishes.

CLOVES Mainly used whole although available ground, cloves have a very warm sweet pungent aroma and can be used to stud roast ham and pork, in mulled wine and punch and when pickling fruit.

CORIANDER Coriander seeds have an orangey flavour and are particularly delicious in casseroles, curries and as a pickling spice. The leaves are used both to flavour spicy aromatic dishes as well as a garnish.

CUMIN Also available ground or as whole seeds, cumin has a strong, slightly bitter flavour. It is one of the main ingredients in curry powder and compliments many fish, meat and rice dishes.

GINGER Ginger comes in many forms but primarily as a fresh root and in dried ground form, which can be used in baking, curries, pickles, sauces and Chinese cooking.

LEMON GRASS Available fresh and dried, with a subtle, aromatic, lemony flavour, lemon grass is essential to Thai cooking. It is also delicious when added to soups, poultry and fish dishes.

MARJORAM Often dried, marjoram has a sweet slightly spicy flavour, which tastes fantastic when added to stuffing, meat or tomato-based dishes.

OREGANO The strongly flavoured dried leaves are similar to marjoram and are used extensively in Italian and Greek cooking.

PAPRIKA Paprika often comes in two varieties. One is quite sweet and mild and the other has a slight bite to it. Paprika is made from the fruit of the sweet pepper and is good in meat and poultry dishes as well as a garnish. The rule of buying herbs and spices little and often applies particularly to paprika as unfortunately it does not keep particularly well.

PARSLEY The stems as well as the leaves of parsley can be used to compliment most savoury dishes as they contain the most flavour. They can also be used as a garnish.

PEPPER This comes in white and black peppercorns and is best freshly ground. Both add flavour to most dishes, sauces and gravies. Black pepper has a more robust flavour, while white pepper has a much more delicate flavour.

ROSEMARY The small needle-like leaves have a sweet aroma which is particularly good with lamb, stuffing and vegetables dishes.

SAFFRON Deep orange in colour, saffron is traditionally used in paella, rice and cakes but is also delicious with poultry.

SAGE The fresh or dried leaves have a pungent slightly bitter taste which is delicious with pork and poultry, sausages, stuffing and with stuffed pasta when tossed in a little butter and fresh sage.

SAVORY This herb resembles thyme, but has a softer flavour that particularly compliments all types of fish and beans.

TARRAGON The fresh or dried leaves of tarragon have a sweet aromatic taste, which is particularly good with poultry, seafood and fish.

THYME Available fresh or dried, thyme has a pungent flavour and is included in bouquet garni. It compliments many meat and poultry dishes and stuffing.

TURMERIC This root is ground and has a brilliant yellow colour. It has a bitter peppery flavour and is often combined for use in curry powder and mustard.

Light Bites

Quick Mediterranean Prawns

SERVES 4

20 raw Mediterranean
    prawns
3 tbsp olive oil
1 garlic clove, peeled
    and crushed
finely grated zest and juice
    of ½ lemon

sprigs of fresh rosemary

For the pesto & sun-dried
    tomato dips:
150 ml/¼ pint Greek
    style yogurt
1 tbsp prepared pesto

150 ml/¼ pint crème fraîche
1 tbsp sun-dried tomato
    paste
1 tbsp wholegrain mustard
salt and freshly ground
    black pepper
lemon wedges, to garnish

Remove the shells from the prawns, leaving the tail shells. Using a small, sharp knife, remove the dark vein that runs along the back of the prawns. Rinse and drain on absorbent kitchen paper.

Whisk 2 tablespoons of the oil with the garlic, lemon zest and juice in a small bowl. Bruise 1 sprig of rosemary with a rolling pin and add to the bowl. Add the prawns, toss to coat, then cover and leave to marinate in the refrigerator until needed.

For the simple dips, mix the yogurt and pesto in one bowl and the crème fraîche, tomato paste and mustard in another bowl. Season to taste with salt and pepper.

Heat a wok, add the remaining oil and swirl round to coat the sides. Remove the prawns from the marinade, leaving any juices and the rosemary behind. Add to the wok and stir-fry over a high heat for 3–4 minutes, or until the prawns are pink and just cooked through.

Remove the prawns from the wok and arrange on a platter. Garnish with lemon wedges and more fresh rosemary sprigs and serve hot or cold with the dips.

Try this: FOR MAIN MEAL: 68   FOR PUDDING: 352

Thai Fish Cakes

SERVES 4

1 red chilli, deseeded and roughly chopped
4 tbsp roughly chopped fresh coriander
1 garlic clove, peeled and crushed
2 spring onions, trimmed and roughly chopped
1 lemon grass, outer leaves discarded and roughly chopped
75 g/3 oz prawns, thawed if frozen
275 g/10 oz cod fillet, skinned, pin bones removed and cubed
salt and freshly ground black pepper
sweet chilli dipping sauce, to serve

Preheat the oven to 190°C/375°F/Gas Mark 5. Place the chilli, coriander, garlic, spring onions and lemon grass in a food processor and blend together.

Pat the prawns and cod dry with kitchen paper.

Add to the food processor and blend until the mixture is roughly chopped.

Season to taste with salt and pepper and blend to mix.

Dampen the hands, then shape heaped tablespoons of the mixture into 12 little patties.

Place the patties on a lightly oiled baking sheet and cook in the preheated oven for 12–15 minutes or until piping hot and cooked through. Turn the patties over halfway through the cooking time.

Serve the fish cakes immediately with the sweet chilli sauce for dipping.

Try this: FOR MAIN MEAL: 86   FOR PUDDING: 362

Fried Whitebait
with Rocket Salad

SERVES 4

450 g/1 lb whitebait,
  fresh or frozen
oil, for frying
85 g/3 oz plain flour
½ tsp of cayenne pepper
salt and freshly ground
  black pepper

For the salad:
125 g/4 oz rocket leaves
125 g/4 oz cherry tomatoes,
  halved
75 g/3 oz cucumber,
  cut into dice
3 tbsp olive oil

1 tbsp fresh lemon juice
½ tsp Dijon mustard
½ tsp caster sugar

If the whitebait are frozen, thaw completely, then wipe dry with absorbent kitchen paper.

Start to heat the oil in a deep-fat fryer. Arrange the fish in a large, shallow dish and toss well in the flour, cayenne pepper and salt and pepper.

Deep fry the fish in batches for 2–3 minutes, or until crisp and golden. Keep the cooked fish warm while deep frying the remaining fish.

Meanwhile, to make the salad, arrange the rocket leaves, cherry tomatoes and cucumber on individual serving dishes. Whisk the olive oil and the remaining ingredients together and season lightly. Drizzle the dressing over the salad and serve with the whitebait.

Try this: FOR MAIN MEAL: 186   FOR PUDDING: 364

Hot Tiger Prawns with Parma Ham

SERVES 4

½ cucumber,	4 garlic cloves,	black pepper
peeled if preferred	peeled and crushed	6 slices of Parma ham,
4 ripe tomatoes	4 tbsp freshly chopped	cut in half
12 raw tiger prawns	parsley	4 slices flat Italian bread
6 tbsp olive oil	salt and freshly ground	4 tbsp dry white wine

Preheat oven to 180°C/350°F/Gas Mark 4. Slice the cucumber and tomatoes thinly, then arrange on 4 large plates and reserve. Peel the prawns, leaving the tail shell intact and remove the thin black vein running down the back.

Whisk together 4 tablespoons of the olive oil, garlic and chopped parsley in a small bowl and season to taste with plenty of salt and pepper. Add the prawns to the mixture and stir until they are well coated. Remove the prawns, then wrap each one in a piece of Parma ham and secure with a cocktail stick.

Place the prepared prawns on a lightly oiled baking sheet or dish with the slices of bread and cook in the preheated oven for 5 minutes.

Remove the prawns from the oven and spoon the wine over the prawns and bread. Return to the oven and cook for a further 10 minutes until piping hot.

Carefully remove the cocktail sticks and arrange three prawn rolls on each slice of bread. Place on top of the sliced cucumber and tomatoes and serve immediately.

Try this: FOR MAIN MEAL: 114 FOR PUDDING: 358

Warm Swordfish Niçoise

SERVES 4

4 swordfish steaks, about 2.5
   cm/1 inch thick, weighing
   about 175 g/6 oz each
juice of 1 lime
2 tbsp olive oil
salt and freshly ground
   black pepper

400 g/14 oz farfalle
225 g/8 oz French beans,
   topped and cut in half
1 tsp Dijon mustard
2 tsp white wine vinegar
pinch caster sugar
3 tbsp olive oil

225 g/8 oz ripe tomatoes,
   quartered
50 g/2 oz pitted black olives
2 medium eggs, hard boiled
   and quartered
8 anchovy fillets, drained
   and cut in half lengthways

Place the swordfish steaks in a shallow dish. Mix the lime juice with the oil, season to taste with salt and pepper and spoon over the steaks. Turn the steaks to coat them evenly. Cover and place in the refrigerator to marinate for 1 hour.

Bring a large pan of lightly salted water to a rolling boil. Add the farfalle and cook according to the packet instructions, or until 'al dente'. Add the French beans about 4 minutes before the end of cooking time.

Mix the mustard, vinegar and sugar together in a small jug. Gradually whisk in the olive oil to make a thick dressing. Cook the swordfish in a griddle pan or under a hot preheated grill for 2 minutes on each side, or until just cooked through; overcooking will make it tough and dry. Remove and cut into 2 cm/¾ inch chunks.

Drain the pasta and beans thoroughly and place in a large bowl. Pour over the dressing and toss to coat. Add the cooked swordfish, tomatoes, olives, hard-boiled eggs and anchovy fillets. Gently toss together, taking care not to break up the eggs.

Tip into a warmed serving bowl or divide the pasta between individual plates. Serve immediately.

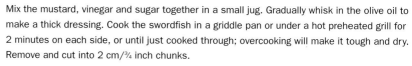

Mixed Salad with Anchovy Dressing & Ciabatta Croûtons

SERVES 4

1 small head endive
1 small head chicory
1 fennel bulb
400 g can artichokes,
    drained and rinsed
½ cucumber
125 g/4 oz cherry tomatoes
75 g/3 oz black olives

For the anchovy dressing:
50 g can anchovy fillets
1 tsp Dijon mustard
1 small garlic clove, peeled
    and crushed
4 tbsp olive oil
1 tbsp lemon juice
freshly ground black pepper

For the ciabatta croûtons:
2 thick slices ciabatta bread
2 tbsp olive oil

Divide the endive and chicory into leaves and reserve some of the larger ones. Arrange the smaller leaves in a wide salad bowl.

Cut the fennel bulb in half from the stalk to the root end, then cut across in fine slices. Quarter the artichokes, then quarter and slice the cucumber and halve the tomatoes. Add to the salad bowl with the olives.

To make the dressing, drain the anchovies and put in a blender with the mustard, garlic, olive oil, lemon juice, 2 tablespoons of hot water and black pepper. Whiz together until smooth and thickened.

To make the croûtons, cut the bread into 1 cm/½ inch cubes. Heat the oil in a frying pan, add the bread cubes and fry for 3 minutes, turning frequently until golden. Remove and drain on absorbent kitchen paper.

Drizzle half the anchovy dressing over the prepared salad and toss to coat. Arrange the reserved endive and chicory leaves around the edge, then drizzle over the remaining dressing. Scatter over the croûtons and serve immediately.

Try this: FOR MAIN MEAL: 120   FOR PUDDING: 350

Crispy Prawns with Chinese Dipping Sauce

SERVES 4

450 g/1 lb medium-sized
  raw prawns, peeled
¼ tsp salt
6 tbsp groundnut oil
2 garlic cloves, peeled
  and finely chopped
2.5 cm/1 inch piece fresh
  root ginger, peeled and

finely chopped
1 green chilli, deseeded
  and finely chopped
4 stems fresh coriander,
  leaves and stems
  roughly chopped

For the Chinese
  dipping sauce:
3 tbsp dark soy sauce
3 tbsp rice wine vinegar
1 tbsp caster sugar
2 tbsp chilli oil
2 spring onions,
  finely shredded

Using a sharp knife, remove the black vein along the back of the prawns. Sprinkle the prawns with the salt and leave to stand for 15 minutes. Pat dry on absorbent kitchen paper.

Heat a wok or large frying pan, add the groundnut oil and when hot, add the prawns and stir-fry in 2 batches for about 1 minute, or until they turn pink and are almost cooked. Using a slotted spoon, remove the prawns and keep warm in a low oven.

Drain the oil from the wok, leaving 1 tablespoon. Add the garlic, ginger and chilli and cook for about 30 seconds. Add the coriander, return the prawns and stir-fry for 1–2 minutes, or until the prawns are cooked through and the garlic is golden. Turn into a warmed serving dish.

For the dipping sauce, using a fork, beat together the soy sauce, rice vinegar, caster sugar and chilli oil in a small bowl. Stir in the spring onions. Serve immediately with the hot prawns.

Fresh Tuna Salad

SERVES 4

225 g/8 oz mixed
   salad leaves
225 g/8 oz baby cherry
   tomatoes, halved
   lengthways
125 g/4 oz rocket leaves,
   washed

2 tbsp groundnut oil
550 g/1¼ lb boned tuna
   steaks, each cut into
   4 small pieces

50 g/2 oz piece fresh
   Parmesan cheese

For the dressing:
8 tbsp olive oil
grated zest and juice of
   2 small lemons
1 tbsp wholegrain mustard
salt and freshly ground
   black pepper

Wash the salad leaves and place in a large salad bowl with the cherry tomatoes and rocket and reserve.

Heat the wok, then add the oil and heat until almost smoking. Add the tuna, skin-side down, and cook for 4–6 minutes, turning once during cooking, or until cooked and the flesh flakes easily. Remove from the heat and leave to stand in the juices for 2 minutes before removing.

Meanwhile make the dressing, place the olive oil, lemon zest and juices and mustard in a small bowl or screw-topped jar and whisk or shake well until well blended. Season to taste with salt and pepper.

Transfer the tuna to a clean chopping board and flake, then add it to the salad and toss lightly.

Using a swivel blade vegetable peeler, peel the piece of Parmesan cheese into shavings. Divide the salad between four large serving plates, drizzle the dressing over the salad, then scatter with the Parmesan shavings.

Sweet & Sour Spareribs

SERVES 4

1.6 kg/3½ lb pork spareribs
4 tbsp clear honey
1 tbsp Worcestershire sauce
1 tsp Chinese five spice
   powder

4 tbsp soy sauce
2½ tbsp dry sherry
1 tsp chilli sauce
2 garlic cloves, peeled
   and chopped

1½ tbsp tomato purée
1 tsp dry mustard powder
   (optional)
spring onion curls,
   to garnish

Preheat the oven to 200°C/400°F/Gas Mark 6, 15 minutes before cooking. If necessary, place the ribs on a chopping board and using a sharp knife, cut the joint in between the ribs, to form single ribs. Place the ribs in a shallow dish in a single layer.

Spoon the honey, the Worcestershire sauce, Chinese five spice powder with the soy sauce, sherry and chilli sauce into a small saucepan and heat gently, stirring until smooth. Stir in the chopped garlic, the tomato purée and mustard powder, if using.

Pour the honey mixture over ribs and spoon over until the ribs are coated evenly. Cover with clingfilm and leave to marinate overnight in the refrigerator, occasionally spooning the marinade over the ribs.

When ready to cook, remove the ribs from the marinade and place in a shallow roasting tin. Spoon over a little of the marinade and reserve the remainder. Place the spareribs in the preheated oven and cook for 35–40 minutes, or until cooked and the outsides are crisp. Baste occasionally with the reserved marinade during cooking. Garnish with a few spring onion curls and serve immediately, either as a starter or as a meat accompaniment.

Try this: FOR MAIN MEAL: 130 FOR PUDDING: 354

Chinese Leaf & Mushroom Soup

SERVES 4-6

450 g/1 lb Chinese leaves
25 g/1 oz dried Chinese
  (shiitake) mushrooms
1 tbsp vegetable oil
75 g/3 oz smoked streaky
  bacon, diced
2.5 cm/1 inch piece fresh

root ginger, peeled and
  finely chopped
175 g/6 oz chestnut
  mushrooms, thinly sliced
1.1 litres/2 pints chicken stock
4–6 spring onions, trimmed
  and cut into short lengths

2 tbsp dry sherry or
  Chinese rice wine
salt and freshly ground
  black pepper
sesame oil for drizzling

Trim the stem ends of the Chinese leaves and cut in half lengthways. Remove the triangular core with a knife, then cut into 2.5 cm/1 inch slices and reserve.

Place the dried Chinese mushrooms in a bowl and pour over enough almost boiling water to cover. Leave to stand for 20 minutes to soften, then gently lift out and squeeze out the liquid. Discard the stems and thinly slice the caps and reserve. Strain the liquid through a muslin-lined sieve or a coffee filter paper and reserve.

Heat a wok over a medium-high heat, add the oil and when hot add the bacon. Stir-fry for 3–4 minutes, or until crisp and golden, stirring frequently. Add the ginger and chestnut mushrooms and stir-fry for a further 2–3 minutes.

Add the chicken stock and bring to the boil, skimming any fat and scum that rises to the surface. Add the spring onions, sherry or rice wine, Chinese leaves, sliced Chinese mushrooms and season to taste with salt and pepper. Pour in the reserved soaking liquid and reduce the heat to the lowest possible setting.

Simmer gently, covered, until all the vegetables are very tender; this will take about 10 minutes. Add a little water if the liquid has reduced too much. Spoon into soup bowls and drizzle with a little sesame oil. Serve immediately.

Try this: FOR MAIN MEAL: 104   FOR PUDDING: 356

Crispy Baked Potatoes
with Serrano Ham

SERVES 4

4 large baking potatoes
4 tsp half-fat crème fraîche
salt and freshly ground
   black pepper
50 g/2 oz lean serrano

ham or prosciutto,
   with fat removed
50 g/2 oz cooked baby
   broad beans
50 g/2 oz cooked carrots, diced

50 g/2 oz cooked peas
50 g/2 oz hard cheese
   such as Edam or
   Cheddar, grated
fresh green salad, to serve

Preheat the oven to 200°C/400°F/Gas Mark 6. Scrub the potatoes dry. Prick with a fork and place on a baking sheet. Cook for 1–1½ hours or until tender when squeezed. (Use oven gloves or a kitchen towel to pick up the potatoes as they will be very hot.)

Cut the potatoes in half horizontally and scoop out all the flesh into a bowl.

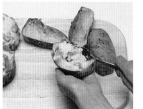

Spoon the crème fraîche into the bowl and mix thoroughly with the potatoes. Season to taste with a little salt and pepper.

Cut the ham into strips and carefully stir into the potato mixture with the broad beans, carrots and peas.

Pile the mixture back into the eight potato shells and sprinkle a little grated cheese on the top.

Place under a hot grill and cook until golden and heated through. Serve immediately with a fresh green salad.

Try this: FOR MAIN MEAL: 106   FOR PUDDING: 358

Bacon & Split Pea Soup

SERVES 4

50 g/2 oz dried split peas
25 g/1 oz butter
1 garlic clove, peeled and finely chopped
1 medium onion, peeled and thinly sliced
175 g/6 oz long-grain rice

2 tbsp tomato purée
1.1 litres/2 pints vegetable or chicken stock
175 g/6 oz carrots, peeled and finely diced
125 g/4 oz streaky bacon, finely chopped

salt and freshly ground black pepper
2 tbsp freshly chopped parsley
4 tbsp single cream
warm crusty garlic bread, to serve

Cover the dried split peas with plenty of cold water, cover loosely and leave to soak for a minimum of 12 hours, preferably overnight.

Melt the butter in a heavy-based saucepan, add the garlic and onion and cook for 2–3 minutes, without colouring. Add the rice, drained split peas and tomato purée and cook for 2–3 minutes, stirring constantly to prevent sticking. Add the stock, bring to the boil, then reduce the heat and simmer for 20–25 minutes, or until the rice and peas are tender. Remove from the heat and leave to cool.

Blend about three-quarters of the soup in a food processor or blender to form a smooth purée. Pour the purée into the remaining soup in the saucepan. Add the carrots to the saucepan and cook for a further 10–12 minutes, or until the carrots are tender.

Meanwhile, place the bacon in a non-stick frying pan and cook over a gentle heat until the bacon is crisp. Remove and drain on absorbent kitchen paper.

Season the soup with salt and pepper to taste, then stir in the parsley and cream. Reheat for 2–3 minutes, then ladle into soup bowls. Sprinkle with the bacon and serve immediately with warm garlic bread.

Soy-glazed Chicken Thighs

SERVES 6-8

900 g/2 lb chicken thighs
2 tbsp vegetable oil
3–4 garlic cloves, peeled
   and crushed
4 cm/1½ inch piece fresh
   root ginger, peeled and

finely chopped or grated
125 ml/4 fl oz soy sauce
2–3 tbsp Chinese rice wine
   or dry sherry
2 tbsp clear honey
1 tbsp soft brown sugar

2–3 dashes hot chilli sauce,
   or to taste
freshly chopped parsley,
   to garnish

Heat a large wok and when hot add the oil and heat. Stir-fry the chicken thighs for 5 minutes or until golden. Remove and drain on absorbent kitchen paper. You may need to do this in 2–3 batches.

Pour off the oil and fat and, using absorbent kitchen paper, carefully wipe out the wok. Add the garlic, with the root ginger, soy sauce, Chinese rice wine or sherry and honey to the wok and stir well. Sprinkle in the soft brown sugar with the hot chilli sauce to taste, then place over the heat and bring to the boil.

Reduce the heat to a gentle simmer, then carefully add the chicken thighs. Cover the wok and simmer gently over a very low heat for 30 minutes, or until they are tender and the sauce is reduced and thickened and glazes the chicken thighs.

Stir or spoon the sauce occasionally over the chicken thighs and add a little water if the sauce is starting to become too thick. Arrange in a shallow serving dish, garnish with freshly chopped parsley and serve immediately.

Try this: FOR MAIN MEAL: 158   FOR PUDDING: 376

Cheesy Chicken Burgers

SERVES 6

1 tbsp sunflower oil
1 small onion, peeled
and finely chopped
1 garlic clove, peeled
and crushed
½ red pepper, deseeded and
finely chopped
450 g/1 lb fresh
chicken mince
2 tbsp 0%-fat Greek yogurt
50 g/2 oz fresh brown
breadcrumbs

1 tbsp freshly chopped
herbs, such as parsley
or tarragon
50 g/2 oz Cheshire
cheese, crumbled
salt and freshly ground
black pepper

For the sweetcorn
and carrot relish:
200 g can sweetcorn,
drained

1 carrot, peeled, grated
½ green chilli, deseeded
and finely chopped
2 tsp cider vinegar
2 tsp light soft brown sugar

To serve:
wholemeal or granary rolls
lettuce
sliced tomatoes
mixed salad leaves

Preheat the grill. Heat the oil in a frying pan and gently cook the onion and garlic for 5 minutes. Add the red pepper and cook for 5 minutes. Transfer into a mixing bowl and reserve. Add the chicken, yogurt, breadcrumbs, herbs and cheese and season to taste with salt and pepper. Mix well. Divide the mixture equally into six and shape into burgers. Cover and chill in the refrigerator for at least 20 minutes.

To make the relish, put all the ingredients in a small saucepan with 1 tablespoon of water and heat gently, stirring occasionally until all the sugar has dissolved. Cover and cook over a low heat for 2 minutes, then uncover and cook for a further minute, or until the relish is thick.

Place the burgers on a lightly oiled grill pan and grill under a medium heat for 8–10 minutes on each side, or until browned and completely cooked through.

Warm the rolls if liked, then split in half and fill with the burgers, lettuce, sliced tomatoes and the prepared relish. Serve immediately with the salad leaves.

Try this: FOR MAIN MEAL: 172   FOR PUDDING: 370

Chicken & Pasta Salad

SERVES 6

450 g/1 lb short pasta
2–3 tbsp extra virgin olive oil
300 g/11 oz cold cooked
   chicken, cut into bite-sized
   pieces (preferably roasted)
1 red pepper, deseeded
   and diced
1 yellow pepper,
   deseeded and diced
4–5 sun-dried tomatoes, sliced

2 tbsp capers, rinsed and
   drained
125 g/4 oz pitted Italian
   black olives
4 spring onions, chopped
225 g/8 oz mozzarella
   cheese, preferably
   buffalo, diced
salt and freshly ground
   black pepper

For the dressing:
50 ml/2 fl oz red or
   white wine vinegar
1 tbsp mild mustard
1 tsp sugar
75–125 ml/ 3–4 fl oz
   extra virgin olive oil
125 ml/4 fl oz mayonnaise

Bring a large saucepan of lightly salted water to the boil. Add the pasta and cook for
10 minutes, or until 'al dente'.

Drain the pasta and rinse under cold running water, then drain again. Place in a large serving
bowl and toss with the olive oil.

Add the chicken, diced red and yellow peppers, sliced sun-dried tomatoes, capers, olives,
spring onions and mozzarella to the pasta and toss gently until mixed. Season to taste with
salt and pepper.

To make the dressing, put the vinegar, mustard and sugar into a small bowl or jug and whisk
until well blended and the sugar is dissolved. Season with some pepper, then gradually whisk
in the olive oil in a slow, steady stream until a thickened vinaigrette forms.

Put the mayonnaise in a bowl and gradually whisk in the dressing until smooth. Pour over the
pasta mixture and mix gently until all the ingredients are coated. Turn into a large, shallow
serving bowl and serve at room temperature.

Oriental Noodle & Peanut Salad with Coriander

SERVES 4

350 g/12 oz rice vermicelli
1 litre/1¾ pints light
   chicken stock
2 tsp sesame oil
2 tbsp light soy sauce
8 spring onions

3 tbsp groundnut oil
2 hot green chillis, deseeded
   and thinly sliced
25 g/1 oz roughly
   chopped coriander
2 tbsp freshly chopped mint

125 g/4 oz cucumber, finely
   chopped
40 g/1½ oz beansprouts
40 g/1½ oz roasted peanuts,
   roughly chopped

Put the noodles into a large bowl. Bring the stock to the boil and immediately pour over the noodles. Leave to soak for 4 minutes, or according to the packet directions. Drain well, discarding the stock or saving it for another use. Mix together the sesame oil and soy sauce and pour over the hot noodles. Toss well to coat and leave until cold.

Trim and thinly slice 4 of the spring onions. Heat the oil in a wok over a low heat. Add the spring onions and, as soon as they sizzle, remove from the heat and leave to cool. When cold, toss with the noodles.

On a chopping board, cut the remaining spring onions lengthways 4–6 times, leave in a bowl of cold water until tassels form. Serve the noodles in individual bowls, each dressed with a little chilli, coriander, mint, cucumber, beansprouts and peanuts. Garnish with the spring onion tassels and serve.

Try this: FOR MAIN MEAL: 182   FOR PUDDING: 352

Tortellini, Cherry Tomato & Mozzarella Skewers

SERVES 6

250 g/9 oz mixed green and plain cheese or vegetable-filled fresh tortellini
150 ml/¼ pint extra virgin olive oil

2 garlic cloves, peeled and crushed
pinch dried thyme or basil
salt and freshly ground black pepper
225 g/8 oz cherry tomatoes

450 g/1 lb mozzarella, cut into 2.5 cm/1 inch cubes
basil leaves, to garnish
dressed salad leaves, to serve

Preheat the grill and line a grill pan with tinfoil, just before cooking. Bring a large pan of lightly salted water to a rolling boil. Add the tortellini and cook according to the packet instructions, or until 'al dente'. Drain, rinse under cold running water, drain again and toss with 2 tablespoons of the olive oil and reserve.

Pour the remaining olive oil into a small bowl. Add the crushed garlic and thyme or basil, then blend well. Season to taste with salt and black pepper and reserve.

To assemble the skewers, thread the tortellini alternately with the cherry tomatoes and cubes of mozzarella. Arrange the skewers on the grill pan and brush generously on all sides with the olive oil mixture.

Cook the skewers under the preheated grill for about 5 minutes, or until they begin to turn golden, turning them halfway through cooking. Arrange two skewers on each plate and garnish with a few basil leaves. Serve immediately with dressed salad leaves.

Try this: FOR MAIN MEAL: 134   FOR PUDDING: 372

Panzanella

SERVES 4

250 g/9 oz day-old Italian-style bread
1 tbsp red wine vinegar
4 tbsp olive oil
1 tsp lemon juice
1 small garlic clove, peeled and finely chopped

1 red onion, peeled and finely sliced
1 cucumber, peeled if preferred
225 g/8 oz ripe tomatoes, deseeded
150 g/5 oz pitted black olives

about 20 basil leaves, coarsely torn or left whole if small
sea salt and freshly ground black pepper

Cut the bread into thick slices, leaving the crusts on. Add 1 teaspoon of red wine vinegar to a jug of iced water, put the slices of bread in a bowl and pour over the water. Make sure the bread is covered completely. Leave to soak for 3–4 minutes until just soft.

Remove the soaked bread from the water and squeeze it gently, first with your hands and then in a clean tea towel to remove any excess water. Put the bread on a plate, cover with clingfilm and chill in the refrigerator for about 1 hour.

Meanwhile, whisk together the olive oil, the remaining red wine vinegar and lemon juice in a large serving bowl. Add the garlic and onion and stir to coat well.

Halve the cucumber and remove the seeds. Chop both the cucumber and tomatoes into 1 cm/½ inch dice. Add to the garlic and onions with the olives. Tear the bread into bite-sized chunks and add to the bowl with the fresh basil leaves. Toss together to mix and serve immediately, with a grinding of sea salt and black pepper.

Try this: FOR MAIN MEAL: 176   FOR PUDDING: 356

Mozzarella Frittata
with Tomato & Basil Salad

SERVES 6

For the salad:
6 ripe but firm tomatoes
2 tbsp fresh basil leaves
2 tbsp olive oil
1 tbsp fresh lemon juice
1 tsp caster sugar
freshly ground black pepper

For the frittata:
7 medium eggs, beaten
salt
300 g/11 oz
    mozzarella cheese
2 spring onions, trimmed
    and finely chopped

2 tbsp olive oil
warm crusty bread,
    to serve

To make the tomato and basil salad, slice the tomatoes very thinly, tear up the basil leaves and sprinkle over. Make the dressing by whisking the olive oil, lemon juice and sugar together well. Season with black pepper before drizzling the dressing over the salad.

To make the frittata, preheat the grill to a high heat, just before beginning to cook. Place the eggs in a large bowl with plenty of salt and whisk. Grate the mozzarella and stir into the egg with the finely chopped spring onions.

Heat the oil in a large, non-stick frying pan and pour in the egg mixture, stirring with a wooden spoon to spread the ingredients evenly over the pan.

Cook for 5–8 minutes, until the frittata is golden brown and firm on the underside. Place the whole pan under the preheated grill and cook for about 4–5 minutes, or until the top is golden brown. Slide the frittata on to a serving plate, cut into six large wedges and serve immediately with the tomato and basil salad and plenty of warm crusty bread.

Try this: FOR MAIN MEAL: 110   FOR PUDDING: 380

Bread & Tomato Soup

SERVES 4

900 g/2 lb very ripe
   tomatoes
4 tbsp olive oil
1 onion, peeled and
   finely chopped
1 tbsp freshly chopped basil

3 garlic cloves, peeled
   and crushed
¼ tsp hot chilli powder
salt and freshly ground
   black pepper
600 ml/1 pint chicken stock

175 g/6 oz stale
   white bread
50 g/2 oz cucumber,
   cut into small dice
4 whole basil leaves

Make a small cross in the base of each tomato, then place in a bowl and cover with boiling water. Allow to stand for 2 minutes, or until the skins have started to peel away, then drain, remove the skins and seeds and chop into large pieces.

Heat 3 tablespoons of the olive oil in a saucepan and gently cook the onion until softened. Add the skinned tomatoes, chopped basil, garlic and chilli powder and season to taste with salt and pepper. Pour in the stock, cover the saucepan, bring to the boil and simmer gently for 15–20 minutes.

Remove the crusts from the bread and break into small pieces. Remove the tomato mixture from the heat and stir in the bread. Cover and leave to stand for 10 minutes, or until the bread has blended with the tomatoes. Season to taste. Serve warm or cold with a swirl of olive oil on the top, garnished with a spoonful of chopped cucumber and basil leaves.

Chinese Omelette

SERVES 1

50 g/2 oz beansprouts
50 g/2 oz carrots, peeled and
   cut into matchsticks
1 cm/½ inch piece fresh root
   ginger, peeled
   and grated

1 tsp soy sauce
2 large eggs
salt and freshly ground black
   pepper
1 tbsp dark sesame oil

To serve:
tossed green salad
soy sauce

Lightly rinse the beansprouts, then place in the top of a bamboo steamer with the carrots. Add the grated ginger and soy sauce. Set the steamer over a pan or wok half-filled with gently simmering water and steam for 10 minutes, or until the vegetables are tender but still crisp. Reserve and keep warm.

Whisk the eggs in a bowl until frothy and season to taste with salt and pepper. Heat a 20.5 cm/8 inch omelette or frying pan, add the sesame oil and when very hot, pour in the beaten eggs. Whisk the eggs around with a fork, then allow them to cook and start to set. When the top surface starts to bubble, tilt the edges to allow the uncooked egg to run underneath.

Spoon the beansprout and carrot mixture over the top of the omelette and allow it to cook a little longer. When it has set, slide the omelette on to a warmed serving dish and carefully roll up. Serve immediately with a tossed green salad and extra soy sauce.

Try this: FOR MAIN MEAL: 180   FOR PUDDING: 354

Rice & Tomato Soup

SERVES 4

150 g/5 oz easy-cook
basmati rice
400 g can chopped tomatoes
2 garlic cloves, peeled
and crushed
grated rind of ½ lime

2 tbsp extra virgin olive oil
1 tsp sugar
salt and freshly
ground pepper
300 ml/½ pint vegetable
stock or water

For the croûtons:
2 tbsp prepared pesto sauce
2 tbsp olive oil
6 thin slices ciabatta
bread, cut into 1 cm/
½ inch cubes

Preheat the oven to 220°C/425°F/Gas Mark 7. Rinse and drain the basmati rice. Place the canned tomatoes with their juice in a large heavy-based saucepan with the garlic, lime rind, oil and sugar. Season to taste with salt and pepper. Bring to the boil, then reduce the heat, cover and simmer for 10 minutes.

Add the boiling vegetable stock or water and the rice, then cook, uncovered, for a further 15–20 minutes, or until the rice is tender. If the soup is too thick, add a little more water. Reserve and keep warm, if the croutons are not ready.

Meanwhile, to make the croutons, mix the pesto and olive oil in a large bowl. Add the bread cubes and toss until they are coated completely with the mixture. Spread on a baking sheet and bake in the preheated oven for 10–15 minutes, until golden and crisp, turning them over halfway through cooking. Serve the soup immediately sprinkled with the warm croutons.

Chicken & Lamb Satay

MAKES 16

225 g/8 oz skinless,
   boneless chicken
225 g/8 oz lean lamb

For the marinade:
1 small onion, peeled
   and finely chopped
2 garlic cloves, peeled
   and crushed
2.5 cm/1 inch piece
   fresh root ginger,

peeled and grated
4 tbsp soy sauce
1 tsp ground coriander
2 tsp dark brown sugar
2 tbsp lime juice
1 tbsp vegetable oil

For the peanut sauce:
300 ml/½ pint coconut milk
4 tbsp crunchy peanut butter
1 tbsp Thai fish sauce

1 tsp lime juice
1 tbsp chilli powder
1 tbsp brown sugar
salt and freshly ground
   black pepper

To garnish:
sprigs of fresh coriander
lime wedges

Preheat the grill just before cooking. Soak the bamboo skewers for 30 minutes before required. Cut the chicken and lamb into thin strips, about 7.5 cm/3 inches long and place in two shallow dishes. Blend all the marinade ingredients together, then pour half over the chicken and half over the lamb. Stir until lightly coated, then cover with clingfilm and leave to marinate in the refrigerator for at least 2 hours, turning occasionally.

Remove the chicken and lamb from the marinade and thread on to the skewers. Reserve the marinade. Cook under the preheated grill for 8–10 minutes or until cooked, turning and brushing with the marinade.

Meanwhile, make the peanut sauce. Blend the coconut milk with the peanut butter, fish sauce, lime juice, chilli powder and sugar. Pour into a saucepan and cook gently for 5 minutes, stirring occasionally, then season to taste with salt and pepper. Garnish with coriander sprigs and lime wedges and serve the satays with the prepared sauce.

Try this: FOR MAIN MEAL: 190   FOR PUDDING: 376

Potato & Fennel Soup

SERVES 4

25 g/1 oz butter
2 large onions, peeled
and thinly sliced
2–3 garlic cloves, peeled
and crushed
1 tsp salt
2 medium potatoes (about

450 g/1 lb in weight),
peeled and diced
1 fennel bulb, trimmed
and finely chopped
½ tsp caraway seeds
1 litre/1¾ pints
vegetable stock

freshly ground
black pepper
2 tbsp freshly
chopped parsley
4 tbsp crème fraîche
roughly torn pieces of
French stick, to serve

Melt the butter in a large, heavy-based saucepan. Add the onions, with the garlic and half the salt, and cook over a medium heat, stirring occasionally, for 7–10 minutes, or until the onions are very soft and beginning to turn brown.

Add the potatoes, fennel bulb, caraway seeds and the remaining salt. Cook for about 5 minutes, then pour in the vegetable stock. Bring to the boil, partially cover and simmer for 15–20 minutes, or until the potatoes are tender. Stir in the chopped parsley and adjust the seasoning to taste.

For a smooth-textured soup, allow to cool slightly then pour into a food processor or blender and blend until smooth. Reheat the soup gently, then ladle into individual soup bowls. For a chunky soup, omit this blending stage and ladle straight from the saucepan into soup bowls. 4Swirl a spoonful of crème fraîche into each bowl and serve immediately with roughly-torn pieces of French stick.

Try this: FOR MAIN MEAL: 150   FOR PUDDING: 352

Main Meals

Mediterranean Fish Stew

SERVES 4-6

4 tbsp olive oil
1 onion, peeled and
  finely sliced
5 garlic cloves, peeled
  and finely sliced
1 fennel bulb, trimmed
  and finely chopped
3 celery sticks, trimmed
  and finely chopped

400 g can chopped tomatoes
  with Italian herbs
1 tbsp freshly
  chopped oregano
1 bay leaf
zest and juice of 1 orange
1 tsp saffron strands
750 ml/1¼ pints fish stock
3 tbsp dry vermouth

salt and freshly ground
  black pepper
225 g/8 oz thick
  haddock fillets
225 g/8 oz sea bass
  or bream fillets
225 g/8 oz raw tiger
  prawns, peeled
crusty bread, to serve

Heat the olive oil in a large saucepan. Add the onion, garlic, fennel and celery and cook over a low heat for 15 minutes, stirring frequently until the vegetables are soft and just beginning to turn brown.

Add the canned tomatoes with their juice, oregano, bay leaf, orange zest and juice with the saffron strands. Bring to the boil, then reduce the heat and simmer for 5 minutes. Add the fish stock, vermouth and season to taste with salt and pepper. Bring to the boil. Reduce the heat and simmer for 20 minutes.

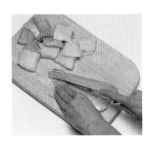

Wipe or rinse the haddock and bass fillets and remove as many of the bones as possible. Place on a chopping board and cut into 5 cm/2 inch cubes. Add to the saucepan and cook for 3 minutes. Add the prawns and cook for a further 5 minutes. Adjust the seasoning to taste and serve with crusty bread.

Try this: FOR STARTERS: 18 FOR PUDDING: 352

Pea & Prawn Risotto

SERVES 6

450 g/1 lb whole raw prawns
125 g/4 oz butter
1 red onion, peeled
and chopped
4 garlic cloves, peeled

and finely chopped
225 g/8 oz Arborio rice
150 ml/¼ pint dry white wine
1.1 litres/2 pints vegetable
or fish stock

375 g/13 oz frozen peas
4 tbsp freshly
chopped mint
salt and freshly ground
black pepper

Peel the prawns and reserve the heads and shells. Remove the black vein from the back of each prawn, then wash and dry on absorbent kitchen paper. Melt half the butter in a large frying pan, add the prawns' heads and shells and fry, stirring occasionally for 3–4 minutes, or until golden. Strain the butter, discard the heads and shells and return the butter to the pan.

Add a further 25 g/1 oz of butter to the pan and fry the onion and garlic for 5 minutes until softened, but not coloured. Add the rice and stir the grains in the butter for 1 minute, until they are coated thoroughly. Add the white wine and boil rapidly until the wine is reduced by half.

Bring the stock to a gentle simmer, and add to the rice, a ladleful at a time. Stir constantly, adding the stock as it is absorbed, until the rice is creamy, but still has a bite in the centre.

Melt the remaining butter and stir-fry the prawns for 3–4 minutes. Stir into the rice, along with all the pan juices and the peas. Add the chopped mint and season to taste with salt and pepper. Cover the pan and leave the prawns to infuse for 5 minutes before serving.

Try this: FOR STARTERS: 40   FOR PUDDING: 364

Cod with Fennel & Cardamom

SERVES 4

1 garlic clove, peeled
    and crushed
finely grated rind of 1 lemon
1 tsp lemon juice

1 tbsp olive oil
1 fennel bulb
1 tbsp cardamom pods
salt and freshly ground

black pepper
4 x 175 g/6 oz thick
    cod fillets

Preheat the oven to 190°C/375°F/Gas Mark 5. Place the garlic in a small bowl with the lemon rind, juice and olive oil and stir well.

Cover and leave to infuse for at least 30 minutes. Stir well before using.

Trim the fennel bulb, thinly slice and place in a bowl.

Place the cardamom pods in a pestle and mortar and lightly pound to crack the pods.

Alternatively place in a polythene bag and pound gently with a rolling pin. Add the crushed cardamom to the fennel slices.

Season the fish with salt and pepper and place on to four separate 20.5 x 20.5 cm/8 x 8 inch parchment paper squares.

Spoon the fennel mixture over the fish and drizzle with the infused oil.

Place the parcels on a baking sheet and bake in the preheated oven for 8–10 minutes or until cooked. Serve immediately in the paper parcels.

Try this: FOR STARTERS: 20 FOR PUDDING: 354

Gingered Cod Steaks

SERVES 4

2.5 cm /1 inch piece fresh root ginger, peeled	1 tbsp soft brown sugar	25 g/1 oz butter
4 spring onions	4 x 175 g /6 oz thick cod steaks	freshly cooked vegetables, to serve
2 tsp freshly chopped parsley	salt and freshly ground black pepper	

Preheat the grill and line the grill rack with a layer of tinfoil. Coarsely grate the piece of ginger. Trim the spring onions and cut into thin strips.

Mix the spring onions, ginger, chopped parsley and sugar. Add 1 tablespoon of water.

Wipe the fish steaks. Season to taste with salt and pepper. Place on to four separate 20.5 x 20.5 cm/8 x 8 inch tinfoil squares.

Carefully spoon the spring onions and ginger mixture over the fish.

Cut the butter into small cubes and place over the fish.

Loosely fold the foil over the steaks to enclose the fish and to make a parcel.

Place under the preheated grill and cook for 10–12 minutes or until cooked and the flesh has turned opaque.

Place the fish parcels on individual serving plates. Serve immediately with the freshly cooked vegetables.

Try this: FOR STARTERS: 24 FOR PUDDING: 356

Sardines with Redcurrants

SERVES 4

2 tbsp redcurrant jelly
finely grated rind of 1 lime
2 tbsp medium dry sherry
450 g /1 lb fresh
  sardines, cleaned and

heads removed
sea salt and freshly ground
  black pepper
lime wedges,
  to garnish

To serve:
fresh redcurrants
fresh green salad

Preheat the grill and line the grill rack with tinfoil 2–3 minutes before cooking.

Warm the redcurrant jelly in a bowl standing over a pan of gently simmering water and stir until smooth. Add the lime rind and sherry to the bowl and stir well until blended.

Lightly rinse the sardines and pat dry with absorbent kitchen paper.

Place on a chopping board and with a sharp knife make several diagonal cuts across the flesh of each fish. Season the sardines inside the cavities with salt and pepper.

Gently brush the warm marinade over the skin and inside the cavities of the sardines.

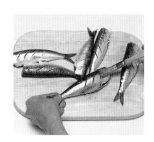

Place on the grill rack and cook under the preheated grill for 8–10 minutes, or until the fish are cooked.

Carefully turn the sardines over at least once during grilling. Baste occasionally with the remaining redcurrant and lime marinade. Garnish with the redcurrants. Serve immediately with the salad and lime wedges.

Try this: FOR STARTERS: 56   FOR PUDDING: 372

Hot Salsa-filled Sole

SERVES 4

8 x 175 g/6 oz lemon
    sole fillets, skinned
150 ml/¼ pint orange juice
2 tbsp lemon juice

For the salsa:
1 small mango

8 cherry tomatoes,
    quartered
1 small red onion, peeled
    and finely chopped
pinch of sugar
1 red chilli
2 tbsp rice vinegar

zest and juice of 1 lime
1 tbsp olive oil
sea salt and freshly ground
    black pepper
2 tbsp freshly chopped mint
lime wedges, to garnish
salad leaves, to serve

First make the salsa. Peel the mango and cut the flesh away from the stone. Chop finely and place in a small bowl. Add the cherry tomatoes to the mango together with the onion and sugar.

Cut the top of the chilli. Slit down the side and discard the seeds and the membrane (the skin to which the seeds are attached). Finely chop the chilli and add to the mango mixture with the vinegar, lime zest, juice and oil. Season to taste with salt and pepper. Mix thoroughly and leave to stand for 30 minutes to allow the flavours to develop.

Lay the fish fillets on a board skinned side up and pile the salsa on the tail end of the fillets. Fold the fillets in half, season and place in a large shallow frying pan. Pour over the orange and lemon juice.

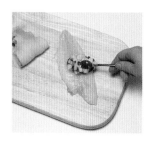

Bring to a gentle boil, then reduce the heat to a simmer. Cover and cook on a low heat for 7–10 minutes, adding a little water if the liquid is evaporating. Remove the cover, add the mint and cook uncovered for a further 3 minutes. Garnish with lime wedges and serve immediately with the salad.

Try this: FOR STARTERS: 30 FOR PUDDING: 380

Zesty Whole–baked Fish

SERVES 8

1.8 kg/4 lb whole
   salmon, cleaned
sea salt and freshly ground
   black pepper
50 g/2 oz low-fat spread
1 garlic clove, peeled
   and finely sliced

zest and juice of 1 lemon
zest of 1 orange
1 tsp freshly grated nutmeg
3 tbsp Dijon mustard
2 tbsp fresh
   white breadcrumbs
2 bunches fresh dill

1 bunch fresh tarragon
1 lime sliced
150 ml/¼ pint half-fat
   crème fraîche
450 ml/¾ pint fromage frais
dill sprigs, to garnish

Preheat the oven to 220°C/425°F/Gas Mark 7. Lightly rinse the fish and pat dry with absorbent kitchen paper. Season the cavity with a little salt and pepper. Make several diagonal cuts across the flesh of the fish and season.

Mix together the low-fat spread, garlic, lemon and orange zest and juice, nutmeg, mustard and fresh breadcrumbs. Mix well together. Spoon the breadcrumb mixture into the slits with a small sprig of dill. Place the remaining herbs inside the fish cavity. Weigh the fish and calculate the cooking time. Allow 10 minutes per 450 g/1 lb.

Lay the fish on a double thickness tinfoil. If liked, smear the fish with a little low fat spread. Top with the lime slices and fold the foil into a parcel. Chill in the refrigerator for about 15 minutes.

Place in a roasting tin and cook in the preheated oven for the calculated cooking time. Fifteen minutes before the end of cooking, open the foil and return until the skin begins to crisp. Remove the fish from the oven and stand for 10 minutes.

Pour the juices from the roasting tin into a saucepan. Bring to the boil and stir in the crème fraîche and fromage frais. Simmer for 3 minutes or until hot. Garnish with dill sprigs and serve immediately.

Try this: FOR STARTERS: 26 FOR PUDDING: 358

Fish Crumble

SERVES 6

450 g/1 lb whiting or
   halibut fillets
300 ml/½ pint milk
salt and freshly ground
   black pepper
1 tbsp sunflower oil
75 g/3 oz butter or margarine
1 medium onion, peeled
   and finely chopped

2 leeks, trimmed and sliced
1 medium carrot, peeled and
   cut into small dice
2 medium potatoes, peeled
   and cut into small pieces
175 g/6 oz plain flour
300 ml/½ pint fish or
   vegetable stock
2 tbsp whipping cream

1 tsp freshly chopped dill
runner beans, to serve

For the crumble topping:
75 g/3 oz butter or margarine
175 g/6 oz plain flour
75 g/3 oz Parmesan
   cheese, grated
¾ tsp cayenne pepper

Preheat the oven to 200°C/400°F/Gas Mark 6, 15 minutes before cooking. Oil a 1.4 litre/ 2½ pint pie dish. Place the fish in a saucepan with the milk, salt and pepper. Bring to the boil, cover and simmer for 8–10 minutes until the fish is cooked. Remove with a slotted spoon, reserving the cooking liquid. Flake the fish into the prepared dish.

Heat the oil and 1 tablespoon of the butter or margarine in a small frying pan and gently fry the onion, leeks, carrot and potatoes for 1–2 minutes. Cover tightly and cook over a gentle heat for a further 10 minutes until softened. Spoon the vegetables over the fish.

Melt the remaining butter or margarine in a saucepan, add the flour and cook for 1 minute, stirring. Whisk in the reserved cooking liquid and the stock. Cook until thickened, then stir in the cream. Remove from the heat and stir in the dill. Pour over the fish.

To make the crumble, rub the butter or margarine into the flour until it resembles bread-crumbs, then stir in the cheese and cayenne pepper. Sprinkle over the dish, and bake in the preheated oven for 20 minutes until piping hot. Serve with runner beans.

 Try this: FOR STARTERS: 64 FOR PUDDING: 370

Roasted Cod with Saffron Aïoli

SERVES 4

For the saffron aïoli:
2 garlic cloves, peeled
¼ tsp saffron strands
sea salt, to taste
1 medium egg yolk
200 ml/7 fl oz extra-virgin
    olive oil
2 tbsp lemon juice

For the marinade:
2 tbsp olive oil
4 garlic cloves, peeled and
    finely chopped
1 red onion, peeled and
    finely chopped
1 tbsp freshly chopped
    rosemary

2 tbsp freshly
    chopped thyme
4–6 sprigs of fresh rosemary
1 lemon, sliced
4 x 175 g/6 oz thick cod
    fillets with skin
freshly cooked vegtables,
    to serve

Preheat the oven to 180°C/350°F/Gas Mark 4, 10 minutes before cooking. Crush the garlic, saffron and a pinch of salt in a pestle and mortar to form a paste. Place in a blender with the egg yolk and blend for 30 seconds. With the motor running, slowly add the olive oil in a thin, steady stream until the mayonnaise is smooth and thick. Spoon into a small bowl and stir in the lemon juice. Cover and leave in the refrigerator until required.

Combine the olive oil, garlic, red onion, rosemary and thyme for the marinade and leave to infuse for about 10 minutes.

Place the sprigs of rosemary and slices of lemon in the bottom of a lightly oiled roasting tin. Add the cod, skinned -side up. Pour over the prepared marinade and leave to marinate in the refrigerator for 15–20 minutes. Bake in the preheated oven for 15–20 minutes, or until the cod is cooked and the flesh flakes easily with a fork. Leave the cod to rest for 1 minute before serving with the saffron aïoli and vegetables.

Salmon & Mushroom Linguine

SERVES 4

450 g/1 lb salmon
   fillets, skinned
salt and freshly ground
   black pepper
75 g/3 oz butter
40 g/1½ oz flour

300 ml/½ pint chicken stock
150 ml/¼ pint
   whipping cream
225 g/8 oz mushrooms,
   wiped and sliced
350 g/12 oz linguine

50 g/2 oz Cheddar
   cheese, grated
50 g/2 oz fresh white
   breadcrumbs
2 tbsp freshly chopped
   parsley, to garnish

Preheat the oven to 190°C/375°F/Gas Mark 5, 10 minutes before cooking. Place the salmon in a shallow pan and cover with water. Season well with salt and pepper and bring to the boil, then lower the heat and simmer for 6–8 minutes, or until cooked. Drain and keep warm.

Melt 50 g/2 oz of the butter in a heavy-based pan, stir in the flour, cook for 1 minute then whisk in the chicken stock. Simmer gently until thickened. Stir in the cream and season to taste. Keep the sauce warm.

Melt the remaining butter, in a pan, add the sliced mushrooms and cook for 2–3 minutes. Stir the mushrooms into the white sauce.

Bring a large pan of lightly salted water to a rolling boil. Add the linguine and cook according to the packet instructions, or until 'al dente'.

Drain the pasta thoroughly and return to the pan. Stir in half the sauce, then spoon into a lightly oiled a 1.4 litre/2½ pint shallow ovenproof dish. Flake the salmon, add to the remaining sauce then pour over the pasta. Sprinkle with the cheese and breadcrumbs, then bake in the preheated for 15–20 minutes, or until golden. Garnish with the parsley and serve immediately.

Try this: FOR STARTERS: 20   FOR PUDDING: 362

Tuna Cannelloni

SERVES 4

1 tbsp olive oil
6 spring onions, trimmed
   and finely sliced
1 sweet Mediterranean
   red pepper, deseeded
   and finely chopped
200 g can tuna in brine

250 g tub ricotta cheese
zest and juice of 1 lemon
1 tbsp freshly snipped chives
salt and freshly ground
   black pepper
8 dried cannelloni tubes
1 medium egg, beaten

125 g/4 oz cottage cheese
150 ml/¼ pint natural yogurt
pinch of freshly grated
   nutmeg
50 g/2 oz mozzarella
   cheese, grated
tossed green salad, to serve

Preheat the oven to 180°C/375°F/Gas Mark 5, 10 minutes before cooking. Heat the olive oil in a frying pan and cook the spring onions and pepper until soft. Remove from the pan with a slotted draining spoon and place in large bowl.

Drain the tuna, then stir into the spring onions and pepper. Beat the ricotta cheese with the lemon zest and juice, and the snipped chives and season to taste with salt and pepper until soft and blended. Add to the tuna and mix together. If the mixture is still a little stiff, add a little extra lemon juice.

With a teaspoon, carefully spoon the mixture into the cannelloni tubes, then lay the filled tubes in a lightly oiled shallow ovenproof dish. Beat the egg, cottage cheese, natural yogurt and nutmeg together and pour over the cannelloni. Sprinkle with the grated mozzarella cheese and bake in the preheated oven for 15–20 minutes, or until the topping is golden brown and bubbling. Serve immediately with a tossed green salad.

Try this: FOR STARTERS: 32   FOR PUDDING: 350

Grilled Red Mullet with Orange & Anchovy Sauce

SERVES 4

2 oranges
4 x 175 g/6 oz red mullet,
    cleaned and descaled
salt and freshly ground
    black pepper
4 sprigs of fresh rosemary

1 lemon, sliced
2 tbsp olive oil
2 garlic cloves, peeled
    and crushed
6 anchovies fillets in
    oil, drained and

roughly chopped
2 tsp freshly chopped
    rosemary
1 tsp lemon juice

Preheat the grill and line the grill rack with tinfoil just before cooking. Peel the oranges with a sharp knife, over a bowl in order to catch the juice. Cut into thin slices and reserve. If necessary, make up the juice to 150 ml/¼ pint with extra juice.

Place the fish on a chopping board and make two diagonal slashes across the thickest part of both sides of the fish. Season well, both inside and out, with salt and pepper. Tuck a rosemary sprig and a few lemon slices inside the cavity of each fish. Brush the fish with a little of the olive oil and then cook under the preheated grill for 4–5 minutes on each side. The flesh should just fall away from the bone.

Heat the remaining oil in a saucepan and gently fry the garlic and anchovies for 3–4 minutes. Do not allow to brown. Add the chopped rosemary and plenty of black pepper. The anchovies will be salty enough, so do not add any salt. Stir in the orange slices with their juice and the lemon juice. Simmer gently until heated through. Spoon the sauce over the red mullet and serve immediately.

Try this: FOR STARTERS: 28 FOR PUDDING: 352

Chilli Monkfish Stir Fry

SERVES 4

350 g/12 oz pasta twists
550 g/1¼ lb monkfish,
   trimmed and cut
   into chunks
2 tbsp groundnut oil
1 green chilli, deseeded
   and cut into matchsticks

2 tbsp sesame seeds
pinch of cayenne pepper
sliced green chillies,
   to garnish

For the marinade:
1 garlic clove, peeled

  and chopped
2 tbsp dark soy sauce
grated zest and juice
  of 1 lime
1 tbsp sweet chilli sauce
4 tbsp olive oil

Bring a large saucepan of lightly salted water to the boil and add the pasta. Stir, bring back to the boil and cook at a rolling boil for 8 minutes, or until 'al dente'. Drain thoroughly and reserve.

For the marinade, mix together the sliced garlic, dark soy sauce, lime zest and juice, sweet chilli sauce and olive oil in a shallow dish, then add the monkfish chunks. Stir until all the monkfish is lightly coated in the marinade, then cover and leave in the refrigerator for at least 30 minutes, spooning the marinade over the fish occasionally.

Heat a wok, then add the oil and heat until almost smoking. Remove the monkfish from the marinade, scraping off as much marinade as possible, add to the wok and stir-fry for 3 minutes. Add the green chilli and sesame seeds and stir-fry the mixture for a further 1 minute.

Stir in the pasta and marinade and stir-fry for 1–2 minutes, or until piping hot. Sprinkle with cayenne pepper and garnish with sliced green chillies. Serve immediately.

Try this: FOR STARTERS: 24   FOR PUDDING: 368

Grilled Snapper with Roasted Pepper

SERVES 4

1 medium red pepper	sea salt and freshly	1 tbsp freshly chopped dill
1 medium green pepper	ground black pepper	sprigs of fresh dill,
4–8 snapper fillets,	1 tbsp olive oil	to garnish
depending on size,	5 tbsp double cream	freshly cooked tagliatelle,
about 450 g/1 lb	125 ml/4 fl oz white wine	to serve

Preheat the grill to a high heat and line the grill rack with tinfoil. Cut the tops off the peppers and divide into quarters. Remove the seeds and the membrane, then place on the foil-lined grill rack and cook for 8–10 minutes, turning frequently, until the skins have become charred and blackened. Remove from the grill rack, place in a polythene bag and leave until cool. When the peppers are cool, strip off the skin, slice thinly and reserve.

Cover the grill rack with another piece of tinfoil, then place the snapper fillets skin-side up on the grill rack. Season to taste with salt and pepper and brush with a little of the olive oil. Cook for 10-12 minutes, turning over once and brushing again with a little olive oil.

Pour the cream and wine into a small saucepan, bring to the boil and simmer for about 5 minutes until the sauce has thickened slightly. Add the dill, season to taste and stir in the sliced peppers. Arrange the cooked snapper fillets on warm serving plates and pour over the cream and pepper sauce. Garnish with sprigs of dill and serve immediately with freshly cooked tagliatelle.

Try this: FOR STARTERS: 18 FOR PUDDING: 356

Chinese Five Spice Marinated Salmon

SERVES 4

700 g/1½ lb skinless
    salmon fillet, cut into
    2.5 cm/1 inch strips
2 medium egg whites
1 tbsp cornflour
vegetable oil for frying
4 spring onions, cut
    diagonally into 5 cm/

2 inch pieces
125 ml/4 fl oz fish stock
lime or lemon wedges,
    to garnish

For the marinade:
3 tbsp soy sauce
3 tbsp Chinese rice wine

or dry sherry
2 tsp sesame oil
1 tbsp soft brown sugar
1 tbsp lime or lemon juice
1 tsp Chinese five
    spice powder
2–3 dashes hot
    pepper sauce

Combine the marinade ingredients in a shallow non-metallic baking dish until well blended. Add the salmon strips and stir gently to coat. Leave to marinate in the refrigerator for 20–30 minutes.

Using a slotted spoon or fish slice, remove the salmon pieces, drain on absorbent kitchen paper and pat dry. Reserve the marinade.

Beat the egg whites with the cornflour to make a batter. Add the salmon strips and stir into the batter until coated completely.

Pour enough oil into a large wok to come 5 cm/2 inches up the side and place over a high heat. Working in 2 or 3 batches, add the salmon strips and cook for 1–2 minutes or until golden. Remove from the wok with a slotted spoon and drain on absorbent kitchen paper. Reserve.

Discard the hot oil and wipe the wok clean. Add the marinade, spring onions and stock to the wok. Bring to the boil and simmer for 1 minute. Add the salmon strips and stir-fry gently until coated in the sauce. Spoon into a warmed shallow serving dish, garnish with the lime or lemon wedges and serve immediately.

Try this: FOR STARTERS: 36 FOR PUDDING: 374

Saucy Cod & Pasta Bake

SERVES 4

450 g/1 lb cod fillets, skinned
2 tbsp sunflower oil
1 onion, peeled and chopped
4 rashers smoked streaky
  bacon, rind removed
  and chopped
150 g/5 oz baby button
  mushrooms, wiped
2 celery sticks, trimmed
  and thinly sliced

2 small courgettes,
  halved lengthwise
  and sliced
400 g can chopped tomatoes
100 ml/3½ fl oz fish stock
  or dry white wine
1 tbsp freshly
  chopped tarragon
salt and freshly ground
  black pepper

For the pasta topping:
225–275 g/8–10 oz pasta shells
25 g/1 oz butter
4 tbsp plain flour
450 ml/¾ pint milk

Preheat the oven to 200°C/400°F/Gas Mark 6, 15 minutes before cooking. Cut the cod into bite-sized pieces and reserve. Heat the sunflower oil in a large saucepan, add the onion and bacon and cook for 7–8 minutes. Add the mushrooms and celery and cook for 5 minutes, or until fairly soft.

Add the courgettes and tomatoes to the bacon mixture and pour in the fish stock or wine. Bring to the boil, then simmer uncovered for 5 minutes, or until the sauce has thickened slightly. Remove from the heat and stir in the cod pieces and the tarragon. Season to taste with salt and pepper, then spoon into a large oiled baking dish.

Meanwhile, bring a large pan of lightly salted water to a rolling boil. Add the pasta shells and cook, according to the packet instructions, or until 'al dente'.

For the topping, place the butter and flour in a saucepan and pour in the milk. Bring to the boil slowly, whisking until thickened and smooth.Drain the pasta thoroughly, and stir into the sauce. Spoon carefully over the fish and vegetables. Place in the preheated oven and bake for 20–25 minutes, or until the top is lightly browned and bubbling.

Try this: FOR STARTERS: 46 FOR PUDDING: 362

Tagliatelle with Tuna & Anchovy Tapenade

SERVES 4

400 g/14 oz tagliatelle
125 g can tuna fish in
   oil, drained
45 g/1¾ oz can anchovy
   fillets, drained

150 g/5 oz pitted black olives
2 tbsp capers in
   brine, drained
2 tsp lemon juice
100 ml/3½ fl oz olive oil

2 tbsp freshly
   chopped parsley
freshly ground black pepper
sprigs of flat-leaf parsley,
   to garnish

Bring a large pan of lightly salted water to a rolling boil. Add the tagliatelle and cook according to the packet instructions, or until 'al dente'.

Meanwhile, place the tuna fish, anchovy fillets, olives and capers in a food processor with the lemon juice and 2 tablespoons of the olive oil and blend for a few seconds until roughly chopped.

With the motor running, pour in the remaining olive oil in a steady stream; the resulting mixture should be slightly chunky rather than smooth.

Spoon the sauce into a bowl, stir in the chopped parsley and season to taste with black pepper. Check the taste of the sauce and add a little more lemon juice, if required.

Drain the pasta thoroughly. Pour the sauce into the pan and cook over a low heat for 1–2 minutes to warm through.

Return the drained pasta to the pan and mix together with the sauce. Tip into a warmed serving bowl or spoon on to warm individual plates. Garnish with sprigs of flat-leaf parsley and serve immediately.

Try this: FOR STARTERS: 32   FOR PUDDING: 352

Hot Prawn Noodles with Sesame Dressing

SERVES 4

600 ml/1 pint vegetable stock	1 red chilli, deseeded and	cooked prawns
350 g/12 oz Chinese	finely chopped	3 tbsp freshly chopped
egg noodles	3 tbsp sesame seeds	coriander
1 tbsp sunflower oil	3 tbsp dark soy sauce	freshly ground black pepper
1 garlic clove, peeled and	2 tbsp sesame oil	fresh coriander sprigs,
very finely chopped	175 g/6 oz shelled	to garnish

Pour the vegetable stock into a large saucepan and bring to the boil. Add the egg noodles, stir once, then cook according to the packet instructions, usually about 3 minutes.

Meanwhile, heat the sunflower oil in a small frying pan. Add the chopped garlic and chilli and cook gently for a few seconds. Add the sesame seeds and cook, stirring continuously, for 1 minute, or until golden.

Add the soy sauce, sesame oil and prawns to the frying pan. Continue cooking for a few seconds, until the mixture is just starting to bubble, then remove immediately from the heat.

Drain the noodles thoroughly and return to the pan. Add the prawns in the dressing mixture, and the chopped coriander and season to taste with black pepper. Toss gently to coat the noodles with the hot dressing.

Tip into a warmed serving bowl or spoon on to individual plates and serve immediately, garnished with sprigs of fresh coriander.

Chinese–style Fried Rice

SERVES 4-6

2–3 tbsp groundnut oil or vegetable oil

2 small onions, peeled and cut into wedges

2 garlic cloves, peeled and thinly sliced

2.5 cm/1 inch piece of fresh root ginger, peeled and cut into thin slivers

225 g/8 oz cooked chicken, thinly sliced

125 g/4 oz cooked ham, thinly sliced

350 g/12 oz cooked cold long-grain white rice

125 g/4 oz canned water chestnuts, sliced

225 g/8 oz cooked peeled prawns (optional)

3 large eggs

3 tsp sesame oil

salt and freshly ground black pepper

6 spring onions, trimmed and sliced into 1 cm/ ½ inch pieces

2 tbsp dark soy sauce

1 tbsp sweet chilli sauce

2 tbsp freshly chopped coriander

To garnish:

2 tbsp chopped roasted peanuts

sprig of fresh coriander

Heat a wok or large deep frying pan until very hot, add the oil and heat for 30 seconds. Add the onions and stir-fry for 2 minutes. Stir in the garlic and ginger and cook for 1 minute. Add the cooked sliced chicken and ham and stir-fry for a further 2–3 minutes.

Add the rice, the water chestnuts and prawns, if using, with 2 tablespoons of water, and stir-fry for 2 minutes until the rice is heated through.

Beat the eggs with 1 teaspoon of the sesame oil and season to taste with salt and pepper. Make a well in the centre of the rice, then pour in the egg mixture and stir immediately, gradually drawing the rice mixture into the egg, until the egg is cooked.

Add the spring onions, soy and chilli sauces, coriander and a little water, if necessary. Adjust the seasoning and drizzle with the remaining sesame oil. Sprinkle with the nuts and serve.

Try this: FOR STARTERS: 48   FOR PUDDING: 354

Oven–roasted Vegetables with Sausages

SERVES 4

2 medium aubergines, trimmed
3 medium courgettes, trimmed
4 tbsp olive oil
6 garlic cloves

8 Tuscany-style sausages
4 plum tomatoes
2 x 300 g cans cannellini beans
salt and freshly ground black pepper

1 bunch of fresh basil, torn into coarse pieces
4 tbsp Parmesan cheese, grated

Preheat the oven to 200°C/400°F/Gas Mark 6, 15 minutes before cooking. Cut the aubergines and courgettes into bite-sized chunks. Place the olive oil in a large roasting tin and heat in the preheated oven for 3 minutes, or until very hot. Add the aubergines, courgettes and garlic cloves, then stir until coated in the hot oil and cook in the oven for 10 minutes.

Remove the roasting tin from the oven and stir. Lightly prick the sausages, add to the roasting tin and return to the oven. Continue to roast for a further 20 minutes, turning once during cooking, until the vegetables are tender and the sausages are golden brown.

Meanwhile, roughly chop the plum tomatoes and drain the cannellini beans. Remove the sausages from the oven and stir in the tomatoes and cannellini beans. Season to taste with salt and pepper, then return to the oven for 5 minutes, or until heated thoroughly.

Scatter over the basil leaves and sprinkle with plenty of Parmesan cheese and extra freshly ground black pepper. Serve immediately.

Try this: FOR STARTERS: 40   FOR PUDDING: 356

Pork Sausages with Onion Gravy & Best–ever Mash

SERVES 4

50 g/2 oz butter
1 tbsp olive oil
2 large onions, peeled
   and thinly sliced
pinch of sugar
1 tbsp freshly chopped thyme
1 tbsp plain flour
100 ml/3½ fl oz Madeira

200 ml/7 fl oz vegetable stock
8–12 good-quality
   butchers pork sausages,
   depending on size

For the mash:
900 g/2 lb floury
   potatoes, peeled

75 g/3 oz butter
4 tbsp crème fraîche or
   soured cream
salt and freshly ground
   black pepper

Melt the butter with the oil and add the onions. Cover and cook gently for about 20 minutes until the onions have collapsed. Add the sugar and stir well. Uncover and continue to cook, stirring often, until the onions are very soft and golden. Add the thyme, stir well, then add the flour, stirring. Gradually add the Madeira and the stock. Bring to the boil and simmer gently for 10 minutes.

Meanwhile, put the sausages in a large frying pan and cook over a medium heat for about 15–20 minutes, turning often, until golden brown and slightly sticky all over.

For the mash, boil the potatoes in plenty of lightly salted water for 15–18 minutes until tender. Drain well and return to the saucepan. Put the saucepan over a low heat to allow the potatoes to dry thoroughly. Remove from the heat and add the butter, crème fraîche and salt and pepper. Mash thoroughly. Serve the potato mash topped with the sausages and onion gravy.

Try this: FOR STARTERS: 38   FOR PUDDING: 366

Sausage & Redcurrant Pasta Bake

SERVES 4

450 g/1 lb good quality, thick pork sausages
2 tsp sunflower oil
25 g/1 oz butter
1 onion, peeled and sliced
2 tbsp plain white flour
450 ml/¾ pint chicken stock

150 ml/¼ pint port or good quality red wine
1 tbsp freshly chopped thyme leaves, plus sprigs to garnish
1 bay leaf
4 tbsp redcurrant jelly

salt and freshly ground black pepper
350 g/12 oz fresh penne
75 g/3 oz Gruyère cheese, grated

Preheat the oven to 220°C/425°F/Gas Mark 7, 15 minutes before cooking. Prick the sausages, place in a shallow ovenproof dish and toss in the sunflower oil. Cook in the oven for 25–30 minutes, or until golden brown.

Meanwhile, melt the butter in a frying pan, add the sliced onion and fry for 5 minutes, or until golden-brown. Stir in the flour and cook for 2 minutes. Remove the pan from the heat and gradually stir in the chicken stock with the port or red wine.

Return the pan to the heat and bring to the boil, stirring continuously until the sauce starts to thicken. Add the thyme, bay leaf and redcurrant jelly and season well with salt and pepper. Simmer the sauce for 5 minutes. Bring a large pan of salted water to a rolling boil, add the pasta and cook for about 4 minutes, or until 'al dente'. Drain thoroughly and reserve.

Lower the oven temperature to 200°C/400°F/Gas Mark 6. Remove the sausages from the oven, drain off any excess fat and return the sausages to the dish. Add the pasta. Pour over the sauce, removing the bay leaf, and toss together. Sprinkle with the Gruyère cheese and return to the oven for 15–20 minutes, or until bubbling and golden-brown. Serve immediately, garnished with thyme sprigs.

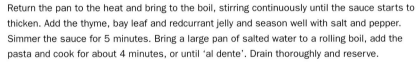

Spanish–style Pork Stew with Saffron Rice

SERVES 4

2 tbsp olive oil
900 g/2 lb boneless pork
    shoulder, diced
1 large onion, peeled
    and sliced
2 garlic cloves, peeled
    and finely chopped
1 tbsp plain flour
450 g/1 lb plum tomatoes,
    peeled and chopped

175 ml/6 fl oz red wine
1 tbsp freshly chopped basil
1 green pepper, deseeded
    and sliced
50 g/2 oz pimiento-stuffed
    olives, cut in half
    crossways
salt and freshly ground
    black pepper
fresh basil leaves, to garnish

For the saffron rice:
1 tbsp olive oil
25 g/1 oz butter
1 small onion, peeled and
    finely chopped
few strands of
    saffron, crushed
250 g/9 oz long-grain
    white rice
600 ml/1 pint chicken stock

Preheat the oven to 150˚C/300˚F/Gas Mark 2. Heat the oil in a large flameproof casserole dish and add the pork in batches. Fry over a high heat until browned. Transfer to a plate until all the pork is browned.

Lower the heat and add the onion to the casserole. Cook for a further 5 minutes until soft and starting to brown. Add the garlic and stir briefly before returning the pork to the casserole. Add the flour and stir.

Add the tomatoes. Gradually stir in the red wine and add the basil. Bring to simmering point and cover. Transfer the casserole to the lower part of the preheated oven and cook for 1½ hours. Stir in the green pepper and olives and cook for 30 minutes. Season to taste with salt and pepper.

Meanwhile, to make the saffron rice, heat the oil with the butter in a saucepan. Add the onion and cook for 5 minutes over a medium heat until softened. Add the saffron and rice and stir well. Add the stock, bring to the boil, cover and reduce the heat as low as possible. Cook for 15 minutes, covered, until the rice is tender and the stock is absorbed. Adjust the seasoning and serve with the stew, garnished with fresh basil.

Try this: FOR STARTERS: 52   FOR PUDDING: 364

Hot Salami & Vegetable Gratin

SERVES 4

350 g/12 oz carrots	1 tbsp freshly chopped mint	black pepper
175 g/6 oz fine green beans	25 g/1 oz butter	1 small or ½ an olive
250 g/9 oz asparagus tips	150 g/5 oz baby	ciabatta loaf
175 g/6 oz frozen peas	spinach leaves	75 g/3 oz Parmesan
225 g/8 oz Italian salami	150 ml/¼ pint double cream	cheese, grated
1 tbsp olive oil	salt and freshly ground	green salad, to serve

Preheat the oven to 200°C/400°F/Gas Mark 6. Peel and slice the carrots, trim the beans and asparagus and reserve. Cook the carrots in a saucepan of lightly salted, boiling water for 5 minutes. Add the remaining vegetables, except the spinach, and cook for about a further 5 minutes, or until tender. Drain and place in an ovenproof dish.

Discard any skin from the outside of the salami, if necessary, then chop roughly. Heat the oil in a frying pan and fry the salami for 4–5 minutes, stirring occasionally, until golden. Using a slotted spoon, transfer the salami to the ovenproof dish and scatter over the mint.

Add the butter to the frying pan and cook the spinach for 1–2 minutes, or until just wilted. Stir in the double cream and season well with salt and pepper. Spoon the mixture over the vegetables.

Whiz the ciabatta loaf in a food processor to make breadcrumbs. Stir in the Parmesan cheese and sprinkle over the vegetables. Bake in the preheated oven for 20 minutes, until golden and heated through. Serve with a green salad.

Antipasto Penne

SERVES 4

3 medium courgettes, trimmed	black pepper	125 g/4 oz Gorgonzola cheese, crumbled
4 plum tomatoes	350 g/12 oz dried penne pasta	3 tbsp freshly chopped flat-leaf parsley
175 g/6 oz Italian ham	285 g jar antipasto	
2 tbsp olive oil	125 g/4 oz mozzarella cheese, drained and diced	
salt and freshly ground		

Preheat the grill just before cooking. Cut the courgettes into thick slices. Rinse the tomatoes and cut into quarters, then cut the ham into strips. Pour the oil into a baking dish and place under the grill for 2 minutes, or until almost smoking. Remove from the grill and stir in the courgettes. Return to the grill and cook for 8 minutes, stirring occasionally. Remove from the grill and add the tomatoes and cook for a further 3 minutes.

Add the ham to the baking dish and cook under the grill for 4 minutes, until all the vegetables are charred and the ham is brown. Season to taste with salt and pepper.

Meanwhile, plunge the pasta into a large saucepan of lightly salted, boiling water, return to a rolling boil, stir and cook for 8 minutes, or until 'al dente'. Drain well and return to the saucepan.

Stir the antipasto into the vegetables and cook under the grill for 2 minutes, or until heated through. Add the cooked pasta and toss together gently with the remaining ingredients. Grill for a further 4 minutes, then serve immediately.

Try this: FOR STARTERS: 46   FOR PUDDING: 380

Chorizo with Pasta in a Tomato Sauce

SERVES 4

25 g/1 oz butter
2 tbsp olive oil
2 large onions, peeled
and finely sliced
1 tsp soft brown sugar
2 garlic cloves, peeled
and crushed

225 g/8 oz chorizo,
sliced
1 chilli, deseeded and
finely sliced
400g can chopped tomatoes
1 tbsp sun-dried
tomato paste

150 ml/¼ pint red wine
salt and freshly ground
black pepper
450 g/1 lb rigatoni
freshly chopped parsley,
to garnish

Melt the butter with the olive oil in a large heavy-based pan. Add the onions and sugar and cook over a very low heat, stirring occasionally, for 15 minutes, or until soft and starting to caramelize.

Add the garlic and chorizo to the pan and cook for 5 minutes. Stir in the chilli, chopped tomatoes and tomato paste, and pour in the wine. Season well with salt and pepper. Bring to the boil, cover, reduce the heat and simmer for 30 minutes, stirring occasionally. Remove the lid and simmer for a further 10 minutes, or until the sauce starts to thicken.

Meanwhile, bring a large pan of lightly salted water to a rolling boil. Add the pasta and cook according to the packet instructions, or until 'al dente'.

Drain the pasta, reserving 2 tablespoons of the water, and return to the pan. Add the chorizo sauce with the reserved cooking water and toss gently until the pasta is evenly covered. Tip into a warmed serving dish, sprinkle with the parsley and serve immediately.

Try this: FOR STARTERS: 54   FOR PUDDING: 370

Penne with Artichokes, Bacon & Mushrooms

SERVES 6

2 tbsp olive oil
75 g/3 oz smoked bacon
or pancetta, chopped
1 small onion, peeled
and finely sliced
125 g/4 oz chestnut
mushrooms, wiped
and sliced
2 garlic cloves, peeled

and finely chopped
400 g/14 oz can artichoke
hearts, drained and halved
or quartered if large
100 ml/3½ fl oz
dry white wine
100 ml/3½ fl oz
chicken stock
3 tbsp double cream

50 g/2 oz freshly grated
Parmesan cheese,
plus extra to serve
salt and freshly
ground black pepper
450 g/1 lb penne
shredded basil leaves,
to garnish

Heat the olive oil in a frying pan and add the pancetta or bacon and the onion. Cook over a medium heat for 8–10 minutes, or until the bacon is crisp and the onion is just golden. Add the mushrooms and garlic and cook for a further 5 minutes, or until softened.

Add the artichoke hearts to the mushroom mixture and cook for 3–4 minutes. Pour in the wine, bring to the boil then simmer rapidly until the liquid is reduced and syrupy.

Pour in the chicken stock, bring to the boil then simmer rapidly for about 5 minutes, or until slightly reduced. Reduce the heat slightly, then slowly stir in the double cream and Parmesan cheese. Season the sauce to taste with salt and pepper.

Meanwhile, bring a large pan of lightly salted water to a rolling boil. Add the pasta and cook according to the packet instructions, or until 'al dente'.

Drain the pasta thoroughly and transfer to a large warmed serving dish. Pour over the sauce and toss together. Garnish with shredded basil and serve with extra Parmesan cheese.

Try this: FOR STARTERS: 36   FOR PUDDING: 376

Gammon with Red Wine Sauce & Pasta

SERVES 2

25 g/1 oz butter
150 ml/¼ pint red wine
4 red onions, peeled
and sliced
4 tbsp orange juice

1 tsp soft brown sugar
225 g/8 oz gammon
steak, trimmed
freshly ground black pepper
175 g/6 oz fusilli

3 tbsp wholegrain mustard
2 tbsp freshly chopped
flat-leaf parsley, plus
sprigs to garnish

Preheat the grill to a medium heat before cooking. Heat the butter with the red wine in a large heavy-based pan. Add the onions, cover with a tight fitting lid and cook over a very low heat for 30 minutes, or until softened and transparent. Remove the lid from the pan, stir in the orange juice and sugar, then increase the heat and cook for about 10 minutes, until the onions are golden.

Meanwhile cook the gammon steak under the preheated grill, turning at least once, for 4–6 minutes, or until tender. Cut the cooked gammon into bite-sized pieces. Reserve and keep warm.

Meanwhile, bring a large pan of very lightly salted water to a rolling boil. Add the pasta and cook according to the packet instructions, or until 'al dente'. Drain the pasta thoroughly, return to the pan, season with a little pepper and keep warm.

Stir the wholegrain mustard and chopped parsley into the onion sauce then pour over the pasta. Add the gammon pieces to the pan and toss lightly to thoroughly coat the pasta with the sauce. Pile the pasta mixture on to two warmed serving plates. Garnish with sprigs of flat-leaf parsley and serve immediately.

Try this: FOR STARTERS: 26   FOR PUDDING: 358

Speedy Pork with Yellow Bean Sauce

SERVES 4

450 g/1 lb pork fillet
2 tbsp light soy sauce
2 tbsp orange juice
2 tsp cornflour
3 tbsp groundnut oil
2 garlic cloves,
peeled and crushed
175 g/6 oz carrots, peeled
  and cut into matchsticks
125 g/4 oz fine green beans,
  trimmed and halved
2 spring onions, trimmed
and cut into strips
4 tbsp yellow bean sauce
1 tbsp freshly chopped flat
  leaf parsley, to garnish
freshly cooked egg noodles,
  to serve

Remove any fat or sinew from the pork fillet, and cut into thin strips. Blend the soy sauce, orange juice and cornflour in a bowl and mix thoroughly. Place the meat in a shallow dish, pour over the soy sauce mixture, cover and leave to marinate in the refrigerator for 1 hour. Drain with a slotted spoon, reserving the marinade.

Heat the wok, then add 2 tablespoons of the oil and stir-fry the pork with the garlic for 2 minutes, or until the meat is sealed. Remove with a slotted spoon and reserve.

Add the remaining oil to the wok and cook the carrots, beans and spring onions for about 3 minutes, until tender but still crisp. Return the pork to the wok with the reserved marinade, then pour over the yellow bean sauce. Stir-fry for a further 1–2 minutes, or until the pork is tender. Sprinkle with the chopped parsley and serve immediately with freshly cooked egg noodles.

Try this: FOR STARTERS: 48   FOR PUDDING: 372

Pork Chop Hotpot

SERVES 4

4 pork chops
flour for dusting
225 g/8 oz shallots, peeled
2 garlic cloves, peeled
50 g/2 oz sun-dried tomatoes
2 tbsp olive oil
400 g can plum tomatoes

150 ml/¼ pint red wine
150 ml/¼ pint chicken stock
3 tbsp tomato purée
2 tbsp freshly chopped
   oregano
salt and freshly ground
   black pepper

fresh oregano leaves,
   to garnish

To serve:
freshly cooked new potatoes
French beans

Preheat the oven to 190°C/375°F/Gas Mark 5, 10 minutes before cooking. Trim the pork chops, removing any excess fat, wipe with a clean, damp cloth, then dust with a little flour and reserve. Cut the shallots in half if large. Chop the garlic and slice the sun-dried tomatoes.

Heat the olive oil in a large casserole dish and cook the pork chops for about 5 minutes, turning occasionally during cooking, until browned all over. Using a slotted spoon, carefully lift out of the dish and reserve. Add the shallots and cook for 5 minutes, stirring occasionally.

Return the pork chops to the casserole dish and scatter with the garlic and sun-dried tomatoes, then pour over the can of tomatoes with their juice.

Blend the red wine, stock and tomato purée together and add the chopped oregano. Season to taste with salt and pepper, then pour over the pork chops and bring to a gentle boil. Cover with a close-fitting lid and cook in the preheated oven for 1 hour, or until the pork chops are tender. Adjust the seasoning to taste, then scatter with a few oregano leaves and serve immediately with freshly cooked potatoes and French beans.

Pork Fried Noodles

SERVES 4

125 g/4 oz dried thread
egg noodles
125 g/4 oz broccoli florets
4 tbsp groundnut oil
350 g/12 oz pork tenderloin,
cut into slices
3 tbsp soy sauce
1 tbsp lemon juice
pinch of sugar

1 tsp chilli sauce
1 tbsp sesame oil
2.5 cm/1 inch piece fresh
root ginger, peeled
and cut into sticks
1 garlic clove, peeled
and chopped
1 green chilli, deseeded
and sliced

125 g/4 oz mangetout, halved
2 medium eggs,
lightly beaten
227 g can water chestnuts,
drained and sliced

To garnish:
radish rose
spring onion tassels

Place the noodles in a bowl and cover with boiling water. Leave to stand for 20 minutes, stirring occasionally, or until tender. Drain and reserve. Meanwhile, blanch the broccoli in a saucepan of lightly salted boiling water for 2 minutes. Drain, refresh under cold running water and reserve.

Heat a large wok or frying pan, add the groundnut oil and heat until just smoking. Add the pork and stir-fry for 5 minutes, or until browned. Using a slotted spoon, remove the pork slices and reserve.

Mix together the soy sauce, lemon juice, sugar, chilli sauce and sesame oil and reserve.

Add the ginger to the wok and stir-fry for 30 seconds. Add the garlic and chilli and stir-fry for 30 seconds. Add the reserved broccoli and stir-fry for 3 minutes. Stir in the mangetout, pork and reserved noodles with the beaten eggs and water chestnuts and stir-fry for 5 minutes or until heated through. Pour over the reserved chilli sauce, toss well and turn into a warmed serving dish. Garnish and serve immediately.

Try this: FOR STARTERS: 34 FOR PUDDING: 374

Hoisin Pork

SERVES 4

1.4 kg/3 lb piece lean belly pork, boned	powder	4 tbsp hoisin sauce
sea salt	2 garlic cloves, peeled and chopped	1 tbsp clear honey
2 tsp Chinese five spice	1 tsp sesame oil	assorted salad leaves, to garnish

Preheat the oven to 200°C/400°F/Gas Mark 6, 15 minutes before cooking. Using a sharp knife, cut the pork skin in a crisscross pattern, making sure not to cut all the way through into the flesh. Rub the salt evenly over the skin and leave to stand for 30 minutes.

Meanwhile, mix together the five spice powder, garlic, sesame oil, hoisin sauce and honey until smooth. Rub the mixture evenly over the pork skin. Place the pork on a plate and chill in the refrigerator to marinate for up to 6 hours.

Place the pork on a wire rack set inside a roasting tin and roast the pork in the preheated oven for 1–1¼ hours, or until the pork is very crisp and the juices run clear when pierced with a skewer.

Remove the pork from the heat, leave to rest for 15 minutes, then cut into strips. Arrange on a warmed serving platter. Garnish with salad leaves and serve immediately.

Try this: FOR STARTERS: 40   FOR PUDDING: 320

Pork with Black Bean Sauce

SERVES 4

700 g/1½ lb pork tenderloin
4 tbsp light soy sauce
2 tbsp groundnut oil
1 garlic clove, peeled
  and chopped
2.5 cm/1 inch piece fresh
  root ginger, peeled and

cut into matchsticks
1 large carrot, peeled
  and sliced
1 red pepper, deseeded
  and sliced
1 green pepper, deseeded
  and sliced

160 g jar black bean sauce
salt
snipped fresh chives,
  to garnish
freshly steamed rice,
  to serve

Using a sharp knife, trim the pork, discarding any fat or sinew and cut into bite-sized chunks. Place in a large shallow dish and spoon over the soy sauce. Turn to coat evenly, cover with clingfilm and leave to marinate for at least 30 minutes. When in the refrigerator ready to use, lift the pork from the marinade, shaking off as much marinade as possible, and pat dry with absorbent kitchen paper. Reserve the marinade.

Heat a wok, add the groundnut oil and when hot, add the chopped garlic and ginger and stir-fry for 30 seconds. Add the carrot and the red and green peppers and stir-fry for 3–4 minutes or until just softened.

Add the pork to the wok and stir-fry for 5–7 minutes, or until browned all over and tender. Pour in the reserved marinade and black bean sauce. Bring to the boil, stirring constantly until well blended, then simmer for 1 minute, until heated through thoroughly. Tip into a warmed serving dish or spoon on to individual plates. Garnish with snipped chives and serve immediately with steamed rice.

Italian Risotto

SERVES 4

1 onion, peeled
2 garlic cloves, peeled
1 tbsp olive oil
125 g/4 oz Italian salami
  or speck, chopped
125 g/4 oz asparagus
350 g/12 oz risotto rice

300 ml/½ pt dry white wine
1 litre/1¾ pints chicken stock,
  warmed
125g/4 oz frozen broad
  beans, defrosted
125g/4 oz Dolcelatte
  cheese, diced

3 tbsp freshly chopped
  mixed herbs, such as
  parsley and basil
salt and freshly ground
  black pepper

Chop the onion and garlic and reserve. Heat the olive oil in a large frying pan and cook the salami for 3–5 minutes, or until golden. Using a slotted spoon, transfer to a plate and keep warm. Add the asparagus and stir-fry for 2–3 minutes, until just wilted. Transfer to the plate with the salami. Add the onion and garlic and cook for 5 minutes, or until softened.

Add the rice to the pan and cook for about 2 minutes. Add the wine, bring to the boil, then simmer, stirring until the wine has been absorbed. Add half the stock and return to the boil. Simmer, stirring until the liquid has been absorbed.

Add half of the remaining stock and the broad beans to the rice mixture. Bring to the boil, then simmer for a further 5–10 minutes, or until all of the liquid has been absorbed.

Add the remaining stock, bring to the boil, then simmer until all the liquid is absorbed and the rice is tender. Stir in the remaining ingredients until the cheese has just melted. Serve immediately.

Try this: FOR STARTERS: 50 FOR PUDDING: 360

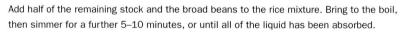

Lamb Pilaf

SERVES 4

2 tbsp vegetable oil
25 g/1 oz flaked or
   slivered almonds
1 medium onion, peeled
   and finely chopped
1 medium carrot, peeled
   and finely chopped
1 celery stalk, trimmed
   and finely chopped
350 g/12 oz lean lamb,

cut into chunks
¼ tsp ground cinnamon
¼ tsp chilli flakes
2 large tomatoes, skinned,
   deseeded and chopped
grated rind of 1 orange
350 g/12 oz easy-cook
   brown basmati rice
600 ml/1 pint vegetable
   or lamb stock

2 tbsp freshly
   snipped chives
3 tbsp freshly
   chopped coriander
salt and freshly ground
   black pepper

To garnish:
lemon slices
sprigs of fresh coriander

Preheat the oven to 140°C/275°F/Gas Mark 1. Heat the oil in a flameproof casserole with a tight-fitting lid and add the almonds. Cook for about 1 minute until just starting to brown, stirring often. Add the onion, carrot and celery and cook gently for a further 8–10 minutes until soft and lightly browned.

Increase the heat and add the lamb. Cook for a further 5 minutes until the lamb has changed colour. Add the ground cinnamon and chilli flakes and stir briefly before adding the tomatoes and orange rind.

Stir and add the rice, then the stock. Bring slowly to the boil and cover tightly. Transfer to the preheated oven and cook for 30–35 minutes until the rice is tender and the stock is absorbed.

Remove from the oven and leave to stand for 5 minutes before stirring in the chives and coriander. Season to taste with salt and pepper. Garnish with the lemon slices and sprigs of fresh coriander and serve immediately.

Try this: FOR STARTERS: 20   FOR PUDDING: 352

Lancashire Hotpot

SERVES 4

1 kg/2¼ lb middle end
    neck of lamb, divided
    into cutlets
2 tbsp vegetable oil
2 large onions,
    peeled and sliced
2 tsp plain flour

150 ml/¼ pint vegetable
    or lamb stock
700 g/1½ lb waxy potatoes,
    peeled and thickly sliced
salt and freshly ground
    black pepper
1 bay leaf

2 sprigs of fresh thyme
1 tbsp melted butter
2 tbsp freshly chopped
    herbs, to garnish
freshly cooked green beans,
    to serve

Preheat the oven to 170°C/325°F/Gas Mark 3. Trim any excess fat from the lamb cutlets. Heat the oil in a frying pan and brown the cutlets in batches for 3–4 minutes. Remove with a slotted spoon and reserve. Add the onions to the frying pan and cook for 6–8 minutes until softened and just beginning to colour, then remove and reserve.

Stir in the flour and cook for a few seconds, then gradually pour in the stock, stirring well, and bring to the boil. Remove from the heat.

Spread the base of a large casserole with half the potato slices. Top with half the onions and season well with salt and pepper. Arrange the browned meat in a layer. Season again and add the remaining onions, bay leaf and thyme. Pour in the remaining liquid from the onions and top with remaining potatoes so that they overlap in a single layer. Brush the potatoes with the melted butter and season again.

Cover the saucepan and cook in the preheated oven for 2 hours, uncovering for the last 30 minutes to allow the potatoes to brown. Garnish with chopped herbs and serve immediately with green beans.

Try this: FOR STARTERS: 38 FOR PUDDING: 366

Marinated Lamb Chops with Garlic Fried Potatoes

SERVES 4

4 thick lamb chump chops
3 tbsp olive oil
550 g/1¼ lb potatoes, peeled
　and cut into
　1 cm/½ inch dice
6 unpeeled garlic cloves
mixed salad or freshly

cooked vegetables,
　to serve

For the marinade:
1 small bunch of fresh
　thyme, leaves removed
1 tbsp freshly

　chopped rosemary
1 tsp salt
2 garlic cloves, peeled
　and crushed
rind and juice of 1 lemon
2 tbsp olive oil

Trim the chops of any excess fat, wipe with a clean damp cloth and reserve. To make the marinade, using a pestle and mortar, pound the thyme leaves and rosemary with the salt until pulpy. Add the garlic and continue pounding until crushed. Stir in the lemon rind and juice and the olive oil.

Pour the marinade over the lamb chops, turning them until they are well coated. Cover lightly and leave to marinate in the refrigerator for about 1 hour.

Meanwhile, heat the oil in a large non-stick frying pan. Add the potatoes and garlic and cook over a low heat for about 20 minutes, stirring occasionally. Increase the heat and cook for a further 10–15 minutes until golden. Drain on absorbent kitchen paper and add salt to taste. Keep warm.

Heat a griddle pan until almost smoking. Add the lamb chops and cook for 3–4 minutes on each side until golden, but still pink in the middle. Serve with the potatoes, and either a mixed salad or freshly cooked vegetables.

Roasted Lamb
with Rosemary & Garlic

SERVES 6

1.6 kg/3½ lb leg of lamb
8 garlic cloves, peeled
few sprigs of fresh rosemary
salt and freshly ground
   black pepper

4 slices pancetta
4 tbsp olive oil
4 tbsp red wine vinegar
900 g/2 lb potatoes
1 large onion

sprigs of fresh rosemary,
   to garnish
freshly cooked ratatouille,
   to serve

Preheat the oven to 200°C/400°F/Gas Mark 6, 15 minutes before roasting. Wipe the leg of lamb with a clean damp cloth, then place the lamb in a large roasting tin. With a sharp knife, make small, deep incisions into the meat. Cut 2–3 garlic cloves into small slivers, then insert with a few small sprigs of rosemary into the lamb. Season to taste with salt and pepper and cover the lamb with the slices of pancetta.

Drizzle over 1 tablespoon of the olive oil and lay a few more rosemary sprigs across the lamb. Roast in the preheated oven for 30 minutes, then pour over the vinegar.

Peel the potatoes and cut into large dice. Peel the onion and cut into thick wedges then thickly slice the remaining garlic. Arrange around the lamb. Pour the remaining olive oil over the potatoes, then reduce the oven temperature to 180°C/350°F/Gas Mark 4 and roast for a further 1 hour, or until the lamb is tender. Garnish with fresh sprigs of rosemary and serve immediately with the roast potatoes and ratatouille.

Try this: FOR STARTERS: 60 FOR PUDDING: 358

Braised Lamb with Broad Beans

SERVES 4

700 g/1½ lb lamb, cut into
large chunks
1 tbsp plain flour
1 onion
2 garlic cloves
1 tbsp olive oil
400 g can chopped tomatoes

with basil
300 ml/½ pint lamb stock
2 tbsp freshly chopped
thyme
2 tbsp freshly chopped
oregano
salt and freshly ground black

pepper
150 g/5 oz frozen
broad beans
fresh oregano,
to garnish
creamy mashed potatoes,
to serve

Trim the lamb, discarding any fat or gristle, then place the flour in a polythene bag, add the lamb and toss until coated thoroughly. Peel and slice the onion and garlic and reserve. Heat the olive oil in a heavy-based saucepan and when hot, add the lamb and cook, stirring until the meat is sealed and browned all over. Using a slotted spoon transfer the lamb to a plate and reserve.

Add the onion and garlic to the saucepan and cook for 3 minutes, stirring frequently until softened, then return the lamb to the saucepan. Add the chopped tomatoes with their juice, the stock, the chopped thyme and oregano to the pan and season to taste with salt and pepper. Bring to the boil, then cover with a close-fitting lid, reduce the heat and simmer for 1 hour.

Add the broad beans to the lamb and simmer for 20–30 minutes, or until the lamb is tender. Garnish with fresh oregano and serve with creamy mashed potatoes.

Spaghetti Bolognese

SERVES 4

1 carrot
2 celery stalks
1 onion
2 garlic cloves
450 g/1 lb lean minced
  beef steak
225 g/8 oz smoked streaky

bacon, chopped
1 tbsp plain flour
150 ml/¼ pint red wine
379 g can chopped tomatoes
2 tbsp tomato purée
2 tsp dried mixed herbs
salt and freshly ground

black pepper
pinch of sugar
350 g/12 oz spaghetti
sprigs of fresh oregano,
  to garnish
shavings of Parmesan
  cheese, to serve

Peel and chop the carrot, trim and chop the celery, then peel and chop the onion and garlic. Heat a large non-stick frying pan and sauté the beef and bacon for 5–10 minutes, stirring occasionally, until browned. Add the prepared vegetables to the frying pan and cook for about 3 minutes, or until softened, stirring occasionally.

Add the flour and cook for 1 minute. Stir in the red wine, tomatoes, tomato purée, mixed herbs, seasoning to taste and sugar. Bring to the boil, then cover and simmer for 45 minutes, stirring occasionally.

Meanwhile, bring a large saucepan of lightly salted water to the boil and cook the spaghetti for 10–12 minutes, or until 'al dente'. Drain well and divide between four serving plates. Spoon over the sauce, garnish with a few sprigs of oregano and serve immediately with plenty of Parmesan shavings.

Try this: FOR STARTERS: 56 FOR PUDDING: 372

Lasagne

SERVES 4

75 g/3 oz butter
4 tbsp plain flour
750 ml/1¼ pints milk
1 tsp wholegrain mustard
salt and freshly ground
  black pepper

¼ tsp freshly
  grated nutmeg
9 sheets lasagne
1 quantity of prepared
  Bolognese sauce
75g/3oz freshly grated

Parmesan cheese
freshly chopped parsley,
  to garnish
garlic bread,
  to serve

Preheat the oven to 200°C/400°F/Gas Mark 6, 15 minutes before cooking. Melt the butter in a small heavy-based pan, add the flour and cook gently, stirring, for 2 minutes. Remove from the heat and gradually stir in the milk. Return to the heat and cook, stirring, for 2 minutes, or until the sauce thickens. Bring to the boil, remove from the heat and stir in the mustard. Season to taste with salt, pepper and nutmeg.

Butter a rectangular ovenproof dish and spread a thin layer of the white sauce over the base. Cover completely with three sheets of lasagne.

Spoon a quarter of the prepared Bolognese sauce over the lasagne. Spoon over a quarter of the remaining white sauce, then sprinkle with a quarter of the grated Parmesan cheese. Repeat the layers, finishing with Parmesan cheese.

Bake in the preheated oven for 30 minutes, or until golden-brown. Garnish with chopped parsley and serve immediately with warm garlic bread.

Italian Beef Pot Roast

SERVES 6

1.8 kg/4 lb brisket of beef
225 g/8 oz small onions, peeled
3 garlic cloves, peeled and chopped
2 celery sticks, trimmed and chopped
2 carrots, peeled and sliced

450 g/1 lb ripe tomatoes
300 ml/½ pint Italian red wine
2 tbsp olive oil
300 ml/½ pint beef stock
1 tbsp tomato purée
2 tsp freeze-dried mixed herbs

salt and freshly ground black pepper
25 g/1 oz butter
25 g/1 oz plain flour
freshly cooked vegetables, to serve

Preheat the oven to 150°C/300°F/Gas Mark 2, 10 minutes before cooking. Place the beef in a bowl. Add the onions, garlic, celery and carrots. Place the tomatoes in a bowl and cover with boiling water. Allow to stand for 2 minutes and drain. Peel away the skins, discard the seeds and chop, then add to the bowl with the red wine. Cover and marinate in the refrigerator overnight.

Lift the marinated beef from the bowl and pat dry with absorbent kitchen paper. Heat the olive oil in a large casserole dish and cook the beef until it is browned all over, then remove from the dish. Drain the vegetables from the marinade, reserving the marinade. Add the vegetables to the casserole dish and fry gently for 5 minutes, stirring occasionally, until all the vegetables are browned.

Return the beef to the casserole dish with the marinade, beef stock, tomato purée, mixed herbs and season with salt and pepper. Bring to the boil, then cover and cook in the preheated oven for 3 hours.

Using a slotted spoon transfer the beef and any large vegetables to a plate and leave in a warm place. Blend the butter and flour to form a paste. Bring the casserole juices to the boil and then gradually stir in small spoonfuls of the paste. Cook until thickened. Serve with the sauce and a selection of vegetables.

Try this: FOR STARTERS: 18   FOR PUDDING: 350

Fillet Steaks with Tomato & Garlic Sauce

SERVES 4

700 g/1½ lb ripe tomatoes
2 garlic cloves
2 tbsp olive oil
2 tbsp freshly chopped basil
2 tbsp freshly

chopped oregano
2 tbsp red wine
salt and freshly ground
   black pepper
75 g/3 oz pitted black

olives, chopped
4 fillet steaks, about 175 g/
   6 oz each in weight
freshly cooked vegetables,
   to serve

Make a small cross on the top of each tomato and place in a large bowl. Cover with boiling water and leave for 2 minutes. Using a slotted spoon, remove the tomatoes and skin carefully. Repeat until all the tomatoes are skinned. Place on a chopping board, cut into quarters, remove the seeds and roughly chop, then reserve.

Peel and chop the garlic. Heat half the olive oil in a saucepan and cook the garlic for 30 seconds. Add the chopped tomatoes with the basil, oregano, red wine and season to taste with salt and pepper. Bring to the boil then reduce the heat, cover and simmer for 15 minutes, stirring occasionally, or until the sauce is reduced and thickened. Stir the olives into the sauce and keep warm while cooking the steaks.

Meanwhile, lightly oil a griddle pan or heavy-based frying pan with the remaining olive oil and cook the steaks for 2 minutes on each side to seal. Continue to cook the steaks for a further 2–4 minutes, depending on personal preference. Serve the steaks immediately with the garlic sauce and freshly cooked vegetables.

Spicy Chilli Beef

SERVES 4

2 tbsp olive oil
1 onion, peeled and
    finely chopped
1 red pepper, deseeded
    and sliced
450 g/1 lb minced beef steak
2 garlic cloves, peeled
    and crushed

2 red chillies, deseeded
    and finely sliced
salt and freshly ground
    black pepper
400 g can chopped tomatoes
2 tbsp tomato paste
400 g can red kidney
    beans, drained

50 g/2 oz good quality, plain
    dark chocolate, grated
350 g/12 oz dried fusilli
knob of butter
2 tbsp freshly chopped
    flat-leaf parsley
paprika, to garnish
soured cream, to serve

Heat the olive oil in a large, heavy-based pan. Add the onion and red pepper and cook for 5 minutes, or until beginning to soften. Add the minced beef and cook over a high heat for 5–8 minutes, or until the meat is browned. Stir with a wooden spoon during cooking to break up any lumps in the meat. Add the garlic and chilli, fry for 1 minute then season to taste with salt and pepper.

Add the chopped tomatoes, tomato paste and the kidney beans to the pan. Bring to the boil, lower the heat, and simmer, covered, for at least 40 minutes, stirring occasionally. Stir in the grated chocolate and cook for 3 minutes, or until melted.

Meanwhile, bring a large pan of lightly salted water to a rolling boil. Add the fusilli and cook according to the packet instructions, or until 'al dente'.

Drain the pasta, return to the pan and toss with the butter and parsley. Tip into a warmed serving dish or spoon on to individual plates. Spoon the sauce over the pasta. Sprinkle with paprika and serve immediately with spoonfuls of soured cream.

Try this: FOR STARTERS: 48   FOR PUDDING: 362

Sweet & Sour Shredded Beef

SERVES 4

350 g/12 oz rump steak
1 tsp sesame oil
2 tbsp Chinese rice wine
   or sweet sherry
2 tbsp dark soy sauce
1 tsp cornflour
4 tbsp pineapple juice
2 tsp soft light brown sugar

1 tsp sherry vinegar
salt and freshly ground
   black pepper
2 tbsp groundnut oil
2 medium carrots, peeled
   and cut into matchsticks
125 g/4 oz mangetout peas,
   trimmed and cut

   into matchsticks
1 bunch spring onions,
   trimmed and shredded
2 garlic cloves, peeled
   and crushed
1 tbsp toasted sesame seeds
freshly cooked Thai fragrant
   rice, to serve

Cut the steak across the grain into thin strips. Put in a bowl with the sesame oil, 1 tablespoon of the Chinese rice wine or sherry and 1 tablespoon of the soy sauce. Mix well, cover and leave to marinate in the refrigerator for 30 minutes.

In a small bowl, blend together the cornflour with the remaining Chinese rice wine or sherry, then stir in the pineapple juice, remaining soy sauce, sugar and vinegar. Season with a little salt and pepper and reserve.

Heat a wok until hot, add 1 tablespoon of the oil, then drain the beef, reserving the marinade, and stir-fry for 1–2 minutes, or until browned. Remove from the wok and reserve.

Add the remaining oil to the wok then add the carrots and stir-fry for 1 minute, then add the mangetout peas and spring onions and stir-fry for a further 1 minute.

Return the beef to the wok with the sauce, reserved marinade and garlic. Continue cooking for 1 minute or until the vegetables are tender and the sauce is bubbling. Turn the stir-fry into a warmed serving dish, sprinkle with toasted sesame seeds and serve immediately with the Thai fragrant rice.

Red Chicken Curry

SERVES 4

225 ml/8 fl oz coconut cream
2 tbsp vegetable oil
2 garlic clove, peeled and
    finely chopped
2 tbsp Thai red curry paste
2 tbsp Thai fish sauce

2 tsp sugar
350 g/12 oz boneless,
    skinless chicken breast,
    finely sliced
450 ml/¾ pint chicken stock
2 lime leaves, shredded

chopped red chilli,
    to garnish
freshly boiled rice
    or steamed Thai
    fragrant rice,
    to serve

Pour the coconut cream into a small saucepan and heat gently. Meanwhile, heat a wok or large frying pan and add the oil. When the oil is very hot, swirl the oil around the wok until the wok is lightly coated, then add the garlic and stir-fry for about 10–20 seconds, or until the garlic begins to brown. Add the curry paste and stir-fry for a few more seconds, then pour in the warmed coconut cream.

Cook the coconut cream mixture for 5 minutes, or until the cream has curdled and thickened. Stir in the fish sauce and sugar. Add the finely sliced chicken breast and cook for 3–4 minutes, or until the chicken has turned white.

Pour the stock into the wok, bring to the boil, then simmer for 1–2 minutes, or until the chicken is cooked through. Stir in the shredded lime leaves. Turn into a warmed serving dish, garnish with chopped red chilli and serve immediately with rice.

Try this: FOR STARTERS: 54   FOR PUDDING: 374

Braised Chicken in Beer

SERVES 4

4 chicken joints, skinned	1 tsp soft dark brown sugar	2 tsp lemon juice
125 g/4 oz pitted	½ tsp whole-grain mustard	2 tbsp chopped fresh parsley
dried prunes	2 tsp tomato purée	flat-leaf parsley, to garnish
2 bay leaves	150 ml/¼ pint light ale	
12 shallots	150 ml/¼ pint chicken stock	To serve:
2 tsp olive oil	salt and freshly ground	mashed potatoes
125 g/4 oz small button	black pepper	seasonal green vegetables
mushrooms, wiped	2 tsp cornflour	

Preheat the oven to 170°C/325°F/Gas Mark 3. Cut each chicken joint in half and put in an ovenproof casserole with the prunes and bay leaves. To peel the shallots, put in a small bowl and cover with boiling water.

Drain the shallots after 2 minutes and rinse under cold water until cool enough to handle. The skins should then peel away easily from the shallots. Heat the oil in a large non-stick frying pan. Add the shallots and gently cook for about 5 minutes until beginning to colour.

Add the mushrooms to the pan and cook for a further 3–4 minutes until both the mushrooms and onions are softened. Sprinkle the sugar over the shallots and mushrooms, then add the mustard, tomato purée, ale and chicken stock. Season to taste with salt and pepper and bring to the boil, stirring to combine. Carefully pour over the chicken. Cover the casserole and cook in the preheated oven for 1 hour. Blend the cornflour with the lemon juice and 1 tablespoon of cold water and stir into the chicken casserole. Return the casserole to the oven for a further 10 minutes or until the chicken is cooked and the vegetables are tender.

Remove the bay leaves and stir in the chopped parsley. Garnish the chicken with the flat-leaf parsley. Serve with the mashed potatoes and fresh green vegetables.

Chicken Baked in a Salt Crust

SERVES 4

1.8 kg/4 lb
   oven-ready chicken
salt and freshly ground
   black pepper
1 medium onion, peeled
sprig of fresh rosemary
sprig of fresh thyme

1 bay leaf
15 g/½ oz butter, softened
1 garlic clove, peeled
   and crushed
pinch of ground paprika
   finely grated rind of
   ½ lemon

To garnish:
fresh herbs, lemon slices
For the salt crust:
900 g/2 lb plain flour
450 g/1 lb fine cooking salt
450 g/1 lb coarse sea salt
2 tbsp oil

Preheat the oven to 170°C/325°F/Gas Mark 3. Remove the giblets if necessary and rinse the chicken with cold water. Sprinkle the inside with salt and pepper. Put the onion inside with the rosemary, thyme and bay leaf.

Mix the butter, garlic, paprika and lemon rind together. Starting at the neck end, gently ease the skin from the chicken and push the mixture under.

To make the salt crust, put the flour and salts in a large mixing bowl and stir together. Make a well in the centre. Pour in 600 ml/1 pint of cold water and the oil. Mix to a stiff dough, then knead on a lightly floured surface for 2–3 minutes. Roll out the pastry to a circle with a diameter of about 51 cm/20 inches. Place the chicken breast side down in the middle. Lightly brush the edges with water, then fold over to enclose. Pinch the joints together to seal.

Put the chicken join side down in a roasting tin and cook in the preheated oven for 2¾ hours. Remove from the oven and stand for 20 minutes.

Break open the hard crust and remove the chicken. Discard the crust. Remove the skin from the chicken, garnish with the fresh herbs and lemon slices. Serve the chicken immediately.

Try this: FOR STARTERS: 48   FOR PUDDING: 356

Slow Roast Chicken with Potatoes & Oregano

SERVES 6

1.4–1.8 kg/3–4 lb oven-ready
  chicken, preferably
  free range
1 lemon, halved
1 onion, peeled and
  quartered

50 g/2 oz butter, softened
salt and freshly ground
  black pepper
1 kg/2¼ lb potatoes,
  peeled and quartered
3–4 tbsp extra-virgin olive oil

1 tbsp dried oregano,
  crumbled
1 tsp fresh thyme leaves
2 tbsp freshly
  chopped thyme
fresh sage leaves, to garnish

Preheat the oven to 200°C/400°F/Gas Mark 6. Rinse the chicken and dry well, inside and out, with absorbent kitchen paper. Rub the chicken all over with the lemon halves, then squeeze the juice over it and into the cavity. Put the squeezed halves into the cavity with the quartered onion.

Rub the softened butter all over the chicken and season to taste with salt and pepper, then put it in a large roasting tin, breast-side down. Toss the potatoes in the oil, season with salt and pepper to taste and add the dried oregano and fresh thyme. Arrange the potatoes with the oil around the chicken and carefully pour 150 ml/¼ pint water into one end of the pan (not over the oil).

Roast in the preheated oven for 25 minutes. Reduce the oven temperature to 190°C/375°F/Gas Mark 5 and turn the chicken breast-side up. Turn the potatoes, sprinkle over half the fresh herbs and baste the chicken and potatoes with the juices. Continue roasting for 1 hour, or until the chicken is cooked, basting occasionally. If the liquid evaporates completely, add a little more water. The chicken is done when the juices run clear when the thigh is pierced with a skewer.

Transfer the chicken to a carving board and rest for 5 minutes, covered with tinfoil. Return the potatoes to the oven while the chicken is resting. Carve the chicken into serving pieces and arrange on a large heatproof serving dish. Arrange the potatoes around the chicken and drizzle over any remaining juices. Sprinkle with the remaining herbs and serve.

Try this FOR STARTERS: 62 FOR PUDDING: 378

Lemon Chicken with Potatoes, Rosemary & Olives

SERVES 6

12 skinless boneless
  chicken thighs
1 large lemon
125 ml/4 fl oz extra-virgin
  olive oil
6 garlic cloves,
  peeled and sliced

2 onions, peeled and
  thinly sliced
bunch of fresh rosemary
1.1 kg/2 ½ lb potatoes,
  peeled and cut into
  4 cm/1½ inch pieces
salt and freshly ground

black pepper
18–24 black olives,
  pitted

To serve:
steamed carrots
courgettes

Preheat the oven to 200°C/400°F/Gas Mark 6, 15 minutes before cooking. Trim the chicken thighs and place in a shallow baking dish large enough to hold them in a single layer. Remove the rind from the lemon with a zester or if using a peeler cut into thin julienne strips. Reserve half and add the remainder to the chicken. Squeeze the lemon juice over the chicken, toss to coat well and leave to stand for 10 minutes.

Transfer the chicken to a roasting tin. Add the remaining lemon zest or julienne strips, olive oil, garlic, onions and half of the rosemary sprigs. Toss gently and leave for about 20 minutes.

Cover the potatoes with lightly salted water and bring to the boil. Cook for 2 minutes, then drain well and add to the chicken. Season to taste with salt and pepper.

Roast the chicken in the preheated oven for 50 minutes, turning frequently and basting, or until the chicken is cooked. Just before the end of cooking time, discard the rosemary, and add fresh sprigs of rosemary. Add the olives and stir. Serve immediately with steamed carrots and courgettes.

Try this: FOR STARTERS: 52 FOR PUDDING: 352

Chicken Parcels with Courgettes & Pasta

SERVES 4

2 tbsp olive oil
125 g/4 oz farfalle pasta
1 onion, peeled and
   thinly sliced
1 garlic clove, peeled
   and finely chopped

2 medium courgettes,
   trimmed and thinly sliced
salt and freshly ground
   black pepper
2 tbsp freshly
   chopped oregano

4 plum tomatoes, deseeded
   and coarsely chopped
4 x 175 g/6 oz boneless,
   skinless chicken breasts
150 ml/¼ pint Italian
   white wine

Preheat the oven to 200°C/400°F/Gas Mark 6, 15 minutes before cooking. Lightly brush four large sheets of non-stick baking parchment with half the oil. Bring a saucepan of lightly salted water to the boil and cook the pasta for 10 minutes, or until 'al dente'. Drain and reserve.

Heat the remaining oil in a frying pan and cook the onion for 2–3 minutes. Add the garlic and cook for 1 minute. Add the courgettes and cook for 1 minute, then remove from the heat, season to taste with salt and pepper and add half the oregano.

Divide the cooked pasta equally between the 4 sheets of baking parchment, positioning the pasta in the centre. Top the pasta with equal amounts of the vegetable mixture, and sprinkle a quarter of the chopped tomatoes over each.

Score the surface of each chicken breast about 1 cm/½ inch deep. Place a chicken breast on top of the pasta and sprinkle each with the remaining oregano and the white wine. Fold the edges of the paper along the top, then along each side, creating a sealed envelope.

Bake in the preheated oven for 30–35 minutes, or until cooked. Serve immediately.

Thai Chicken Fried Rice

SERVES 4

175 g/6 oz boneless,
    chicken breast
2 tbsp vegetable oil
2 garlic cloves, peeled
    and finely chopped
2 tsp medium curry paste

450 g/1 lb cold cooked rice
1 tbsp light soy sauce
2 tbsp Thai fish sauce
large pinch of sugar
freshly ground black pepper

To garnish:
2 spring onions, trimmed
    and shredded lengthways
½ small onion, peeled
    and very finely sliced

Using a sharp knife, trim the chicken, discarding any sinew or fat and cut into small cubes. Reserve.

Heat a wok or large frying pan, add the oil and when hot, add the garlic and cook for 10–20 seconds or until just golden. Add the curry paste and stir-fry for a few seconds. Add the chicken and stir-fry for 3–4 minutes, or until tender and the chicken has turned white.

Stir the cold cooked rice into the chicken mixture, then add the soy sauce, fish sauce and sugar, stirring well after each addition. Stir-fry for 2–3 minutes, or until the chicken is cooked through and the rice is piping hot.

Check the seasoning and, if necessary, add a little extra soy sauce. Turn the rice and chicken mixture into a warmed serving dish. Season lightly with black pepper and garnish with shredded spring onion and onion slices. Serve immediately.

Try this: FOR STARTERS: 30 FOR PUDDING: 364

Cheesy Baked Chicken Macaroni

SERVES 4

1 tbsp olive oil
350 g/12 oz boneless
and skinless chicken
breasts, diced
75 g/3 oz pancetta,
diced
1 onion, peeled
and chopped

1 garlic clove, peeled
and chopped
350 g packet fresh
tomato sauce
400 g can chopped tomatoes
2 tbsp freshly chopped basil,
plus leaves to garnish
salt and freshly ground

black pepper
350 g/12 oz macaroni
150 g/5oz mozzarella cheese,
drained and chopped
50 g/2 oz Gruyère
cheese, grated
50 g/2 oz freshly grated
Parmesan cheese

Preheat the grill just before cooking. Heat the oil in large frying pan and cook the chicken for 8 minutes, or until browned, stirring occasionally. Drain on absorbent kitchen paper and reserve. Add the pancetta slices to the pan and fry on both sides until crispy. Remove from the pan and reserve.

Add the onion and garlic to the frying pan and cook for 5 minutes, or until softened. Stir in the tomato sauce, chopped tomatoes and basil and season to taste with salt and pepper. Bring to the boil, lower the heat and simmer the sauce for 5 minutes.

Meanwhile, bring a large pan of lightly salted water to a rolling boil. Add the macaroni and cook according to the packet instructions, or until 'al dente'.

Drain the macaroni thoroughly, return to the pan and stir in the sauce, chicken and mozzarella cheese. Spoon into a shallow ovenproof dish.

Sprinkle the pancetta over the macaroni. Sprinkle over the Gruyère and Parmesan cheeses. Place under the preheated grill and cook for 5–10 minutes, or until golden-brown; turn the dish occasionally. Garnish and serve immediately.

Try this: FOR STARTERS: 50 FOR PUDDING: 370

Chicken & Baby Vegetable Stir Fry

SERVES 4

2 tbsp groundnut oil
1 small red chilli, deseeded and finely chopped
150 g/5 oz chicken breast or thigh meat, skinned and cut into cubes
2 baby leeks, trimmed and sliced
12 asparagus spears, halved

125 g/4 oz mangetout peas, trimmed
125 g/4 oz baby carrots, trimmed and halved lengthways
125 g/4 oz fine green beans, trimmed and diagonally sliced
125 g/4 oz baby sweetcorn,

diagonally halved
50 ml/2 fl oz chicken stock
2 tsp light soy sauce
1 tbsp dry sherry
1 tsp sesame oil
toasted sesame seeds, to garnish

Heat the wok until very hot and add the oil. Add the chopped chilli and chicken and stir-fry for 4–5 minutes, or until the chicken is cooked and golden.

Increase the heat, add the leeks to the chicken and stir-fry for 2 minutes. Add the asparagus spears, mangetout peas, baby carrots, green beans, and baby sweetcorn. Stir-fry for 3–4 minutes, or until the vegetables soften slightly but still retain a slight crispness.

In a small bowl, mix together the chicken stock, soy sauce, dry sherry and sesame oil. Pour into the wok, stir and cook until heated through. Sprinkle with the toasted sesame seeds and serve immediately.

Try this: FOR STARTERS: 58   FOR PUDDING: 380

Stir-fried Chicken with Basil

SERVES 4

3 tbsp sunflower oil
3 tbsp green curry paste
450 g/1 lb skinless, boneless
    chicken breast fillets,
    trimmed and cut
    into cubes
8 cherry tomatoes

100 ml/4 fl oz coconut cream
2 tbsp soft brown sugar
2 tbsp Thai fish sauce
1 red chilli, deseeded
    and thinly sliced
1 green chilli, deseeded
    and thinly sliced

75 g/3 oz fresh torn
    basil leaves
sprigs of fresh coriander,
    to garnish
freshly steamed white rice,
    to serve

Heat the wok, then add the oil and heat for 1 minute. Add the green curry paste and cook, stirring for 1 minute to release the flavour and cook the paste. Add the chicken and stir-fry over a high heat for 2 minutes, making sure the chicken is coated thoroughly with the green curry paste.

Reduce the heat under the wok, then add the cherry tomatoes and cook, stirring gently, for 2–3 minutes, or until the tomatoes burst and begin to disintegrate into the green curry paste.

Add half the coconut cream and add to the wok with the brown sugar, Thai fish sauce and the red and green chillies. Stir-fry gently for 5 minutes, or until the sauce is amalgamated and the chicken is cooked thoroughly.

Just before serving, sprinkle the chicken with the torn basil leaves and add the remaining coconut cream, then serve immediately with freshly steamed white rice garnished with fresh coriander sprigs.

Try this: FOR STARTERS: 44   FOR PUDDING: 368

Chicken & Cashew Nuts

SERVES 4

450 g/1 lb skinless chicken,
   boneless breast fillets, cut
   into 1 cm/½ inch cubes
1 medium egg white, beaten
1 tsp salt
1 tsp sesame oil
2 tsp cornflour

300 ml/½ pint groundnut
   oil for deep frying
2 tsp sunflower oil
50 g/2 oz unsalted cashews
4 spring onions, shredded
50 g/2 oz mangetout peas,
   diagonally sliced

1 tbsp Chinese rice wine
1 tbsp light soy sauce
shredded spring onions,
   to garnish
freshly steamed white rice
   with fresh coriander
   leaves, to serve

Place the cubes of chicken in a large bowl. Add the egg white, salt, sesame oil and cornflour. Mix well to ensure the chicken is coated thoroughly. Chill in the refrigerator for 20 minutes.

Heat the wok until very hot, add the groundnut oil and when hot, remove the wok from the heat and add the chicken. Stir continuously to prevent the chicken from sticking to the wok. When the chicken turns white, after about 2 minutes, remove it using a slotted spoon and reserve. Discard the oil.

Wipe the wok clean with absorbent kitchen paper and heat it again until very hot. Add the sunflower oil and heat. When hot, add the cashew nuts, spring onions and mangetout peas and stir-fry for 1 minute.

Add the rice wine and soy sauce. Return the chicken to the wok and stir-fry for 2 minutes. Garnish with shredded spring onions and serve immediately with freshly steamed rice sprinkled with fresh coriander.

Stir-fried Chicken with Spinach, Tomatoes & Pine Nuts

SERVES 4

50 g/2 oz pine nuts
2 tbsp sunflower oil
1 red onion, peeled and
    finely chopped
450 g/1 lb skinless, boneless
    chicken breast fillets,
    cut into strips

450 g/1 lb cherry
    tomatoes, halved
225 g/8 oz baby
    spinach, washed
salt and freshly ground
    black pepper
¼ tsp freshly

grated nutmeg
2 tbsp balsamic vinegar
50 g/2 oz raisins
freshly cooked ribbon
    noodles tossed in butter,
    to serve

Heat the wok and add the pine nuts. Dry-fry for about 2 minutes, shaking often to ensure that they toast but do not burn. Remove and reserve. Wipe any dust from the wok.

Heat the wok again, add the oil and when hot, add the red onion and stir-fry for 2 minutes. Add the chicken and stir-fry for 2–3 minutes, or until golden brown. Reduce the heat, toss in the cherry tomatoes and stir-fry gently until the tomatoes start to disintegrate.

Add the baby spinach and stir-fry for 2–3 minutes, or until they start to wilt. Season to taste with salt and pepper, then sprinkle in the grated nutmeg and drizzle in the balsamic vinegar. Finally, stir in the raisins and reserved toasted pine nuts. Serve immediately on a bed of buttered ribbon noodles.

Try this: FOR STARTERS: 52   FOR PUDDING: 354

Chicken with Noodles

SERVES 2–3

225 g/8 oz medium
egg noodles
125 g/4 oz skinless, boneless
chicken breast fillets
1 tbsp light soy sauce
2 tsp Chinese rice wine

or dry sherry
5 tsp groundnut oil
2 garlic cloves, peeled and
finely chopped
50 g/2 oz mangetout peas
25 g/1 oz smoked back

bacon, cut into fine strips
½ tsp sugar
2 spring onions,
peeled and finely
chopped
1 tsp sesame oil

Cook the noodles according to the packet directions. Drain and refresh under cold water. Drain again and reserve.

Slice the chicken into fine shreds and mix with 2 teaspoons of the light soy sauce and Chinese rice wine. Leave to marinate in the refrigerator for 10 minutes.

Heat a wok, add 2 teaspoons of the oil and when hot, stir-fry the chicken shreds for about 2 minutes, then transfer to a plate. Wipe the wok clean with absorbent kitchen paper.

Return the wok to the heat and add the remaining oil. Add the garlic, then after 10 seconds add the mangetout peas and bacon. Stir-fry for a further 1 minute, then add the drained noodles, remaining soy sauce, sugar and spring onions. Stir-fry for a further 2 minutes then add the reserved chicken.

Stir-fry for a further 3–4 minutes until the chicken is cooked through. Add the sesame oil and mix together. Serve either hot or cold.

Try this: FOR STARTERS: 36   FOR PUDDING: 372

Chicken Under a Brick

SERVES 4-6

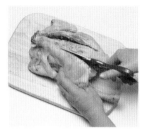

1.8 kg/4 lb free range
   corn-fed,
   oven-ready chicken

50 ml/2 fl oz olive oil
sea salt and freshly
   ground black pepper

To garnish:
sprigs of fresh basil chives
tossed bitter salad leaves,
   to serve

Rinse the chicken and dry well, inside and out. Using poultry shears or kitchen scissors, cut along each side of the backbone of the chicken and discard or use for stock. Place the chicken skin-side up on a work surface and, using the palm of your hand, press down firmly to break the breast bone and flatten the bird.

Turn the chicken breast-side up and use a sharp knife to slit the skin between the breast and thigh on each side. Fold the legs in and push the drumstick bones through the slits. Tuck the wing under, the chicken should be as flat as possible.

Heat the olive oil in a large, heavy-based frying pan until very hot, but not smoking. Place the chicken in the pan, skin-side down, and place a flat lid or plate directly on top of the chicken. Top with a brick (hence the name) or 2 kg/5 lb weight. Cook for 12–15 minutes, or until golden brown. Remove the weights and lid and, using a pair of tongs, turn the chicken carefully, then season to taste with salt and pepper. Cover and weight the lid again, then cook for 12–15 minutes longer, until the chicken is tender and the juices run clear when a thigh is pierced with a sharp knife or skewer.

Transfer the chicken to a serving plate and cover loosely with tinfoil to keep warm. Allow to rest for at least 10 minutes before carving. Garnish with sprigs of basil and chives and serve with salad leaves.

Try this: FOR STARTERS: 42   FOR PUDDING: 356

Mixed Vegetable & Chicken Pasta

SERVES 4

3 boneless and skinless
   chicken breasts
2 leeks
1 red onion
350 g/12 oz pasta shells
25 g/1 oz butter
2 tbsp olive oil

1 garlic clove,
   peeled and chopped
175 g/6 oz cherry tomatoes,
   halved
200 ml/7 fl oz double cream
425 g can asparagus
   tips, drained

salt and freshly ground
   black pepper
125 g/4 oz double Gloucester
   cheese with chives,
   crumbled
green salad,
   to serve

Preheat the grill just before using. Cut the chicken into thin strips. Trim the leeks, leaving some of the dark green tops, then shred and wash thoroughly in plenty of cold water. Peel the onion and cut into thin wedges.

Bring a large pan of lightly salted water to a rolling boil. Add the pasta and cook according to the packet instructions, or until 'al dente'.

Meanwhile, melt butter with the olive oil in a large heavy-based pan, add the chicken and cook, stirring occasionally, for 8 minutes, or until browned all over. Add the leeks and onion and cook for 5 minutes, or until softened. Add the garlic and cherry tomatoes and cook for a further 2 minutes.

Stir the cream and asparagus tips into the chicken and vegetable mixture, bring to the boil slowly, then remove from the heat. Drain the pasta thoroughly and return to the pan. Pour the sauce over the pasta, season to taste with salt and pepper, then toss lightly.

Tip the pasta mixture into a gratin dish and sprinkle with the cheese. Cook under the preheated grill for 5 minutes, or until bubbling and golden, turning the dish occasionally. Serve immediately with a green salad.

Chicken Gorgonzola & Mushroom Macaroni

SERVES 4

450 g/1 lb macaroni
75 g/3 oz butter
225 g/8 oz chestnut
mushrooms, wiped
and sliced
225 g/8 oz baby button
mushrooms, wiped
and halved

350 g/12 oz cooked chicken,
skinned and chopped
2 tsp cornflour
300 ml/½ pint semi-skimmed
milk
50 g/2 oz Gorgonzola
cheese, chopped, plus
extra to serve

2 tbsp freshly chopped sage
1 tbsp freshly chopped
chives, plus extra chive
leaves to garnish
salt and freshly ground
black pepper

Bring a large pan of lightly salted water to a rolling boil. Add the macaroni and cook according to the packet instructions, or until 'al dente'.

Meanwhile, melt the butter in a large frying pan, add the chestnut and button mushrooms and cook for 5 minutes, or until golden, stirring occasionally. Add the chicken to the pan and cook for 4 minutes, or until heated through thoroughly and slightly golden, stirring occasionally.

Blend the cornflour with a little of the milk in a jug to form a smooth paste, then gradually blend in the remaining milk and pour into the frying pan. Bring to the boil slowly, stirring constantly. Add cheese and cook for 1 minute, stirring frequently until melted.

Stir the sage and chives into the frying pan. Season to taste with salt and pepper then heat through. Drain the macaroni thoroughly and return to the pan. Pour the chicken and mushroom sauce over the macaroni and toss lightly to coat. Tip into a warmed serving dish, and serve immediately with extra Gorgonzola cheese.

Try this: FOR STARTERS: 62   FOR PUDDING: 378

Thai Chicken with Chilli & Peanuts

SERVES 4

2 tbsp vegetable or
    groundnut oil
1 garlic clove, peeled
    and finely chopped
1 tsp dried chilli flakes
350 g/12 oz boneless,
    skinless chicken breast,
finely sliced
1 tbsp Thai fish sauce
2 tbsp peanuts, roasted and
    roughly chopped
225 g/ 8 oz sugar snap peas
3 tbsp chicken stock
1 tbsp light soy sauce
1 tbsp dark soy sauce
large pinch of sugar
freshly chopped coriander,
    to garnish
boiled or steamed rice,
    to serve

Heat a wok or large frying pan, add the oil and when hot, carefully swirl the oil around the wok until the sides are lightly coated with the oil. Add the garlic and stir-fry for 10–20 seconds, or until starting to brown. Add the chilli flakes and stir-fry for a few seconds more.

Add the finely sliced chicken to the wok and stir-fry for 2–3 minutes, or until the chicken has turned white.

Add the following ingredients, stirring well after each addition: fish sauce, peanuts, sugar snap peas, chicken stock, light and dark soy sauces and sugar. Give a final stir.

Bring the contents of the wok to the boil, then simmer gently for 3–4 minutes, or until the chicken and vegetables are tender. Remove from the heat and tip into a warmed serving dish. Garnish with chopped coriander and serve immediately with boiled or steamed rice.

Try this: FOR STARTERS: 58   FOR PUDDING: 376

Pesto Chicken Tagliatelle

SERVES 4

2 tbsp olive oil
350 g/12 oz boneless and
  skinless chicken breasts,
  cut into chunks
75 g/3 oz butter
2 medium leeks, trimmed
  and sliced thinly

125 g/4 oz oyster
  mushrooms, trimmed
  and halved
200 g/7 oz small open
  chestnut mushrooms,
  wiped and halved
450 g/1lb fresh tagliatelle

4–6 tbsp red pesto
200 ml/7 fl oz crème fraîche
50 g/2 oz freshly grated
  Parmesan cheese
salt and freshly ground
  black pepper

Heat the oil in a large frying pan, add the chicken and cook for 8 minutes, or until golden-brown, stirring occasionally. Using a slotted spoon, remove the chicken from the pan, drain on absorbent kitchen paper and reserve.

Melt the butter in the pan. Add the leeks and cook for 3–5 minutes, or until slightly softened, stirring occasionally. Add the oyster and chestnut mushrooms and cook for 5 minutes, or until browned, stirring occasionally.

Bring a large pan of lightly salted water to the boil, add the tagliatelle, return to the boil and cook for 4 minutes, or until 'al dente'.

Add the chicken, pesto and crème fraîche to the mushroom mixture. Stir, then heat through thoroughly. Stir in the grated Parmesan cheese and season to taste with salt and pepper.

Drain the tagliatelle thoroughly and pile on to warmed plates. Spoon over the sauce and serve immediately.

Try this: FOR STARTERS: 46   FOR PUDDING: 354

Braised Chicken with Aubergine

SERVES 4

3 tbsp vegetable oil
12 chicken thighs
2 large aubergines,
    trimmed and cubed
4 garlic cloves, peeled
    and crushed
2 tsp freshly grated
    root ginger

900 ml/1½ pints
    vegetable stock
2 tbsp light soy sauce
2 tbsp Chinese preserved
    black beans
6 spring onions, trimmed
    and thinly sliced
    diagonally

1 tbsp cornflour
1 tbsp sesame oil
spring onion tassels,
    to garnish
freshly cooked noodles
    or rice, to serve

Heat a wok or large frying pan, add the oil and when hot, add the chicken thighs and cook over a medium high heat for 5 minutes, or until browned all over. Transfer to a large plate and keep warm.

Add the aubergine to the wok and cook over a high heat for 5 minutes or until browned, turning occasionally. Add the garlic and ginger and stir-fry for 1 minute.

Return the chicken to the wok, pour in the stock and add the soy sauce and black beans. Bring to the boil, then simmer for 20 minutes, or until the chicken is tender. Add the spring onions after 10 minutes.

Blend the cornflour with 2 tablespoons of water. Stir into the wok and simmer until the sauce has thickened. Stir in the sesame oil, heat for 30 seconds, then remove from the heat. Garnish with spring onion tassels and serve immediately with noodles or rice.

Noodles with Turkey & Mushrooms

SERVES 4

225 g/8 oz dried egg noodles
1 tbsp groundnut oil
1 red onion, peeled
 and sliced
2 tbsp freshly grated
 root ginger
3 garlic cloves, peeled and

finely chopped
350 g/12 oz turkey breast,
 skinned and cut into strips
125 g/4 oz baby button
 mushrooms
150 g/5 oz chestnut
 mushrooms

2 tbsp dark soy sauce
2 tbsp hoisin sauce
2 tbsp dry sherry
4 tbsp vegetable stock
2 tsp cornflour

Bring a large saucepan of lightly salted water to the boil and add the noodles. Cook for 3–5 minutes, then drain and plunge immediately into cold water. When cool, drain again and reserve.

Heat the wok, add the oil and when hot, add the onion and stir-fry for 3 minutes until it starts to soften. Add the ginger and garlic and stir-fry for a further 3 minutes, then add the turkey strips and stir-fry for 4–5 minutes until sealed and golden.

Wipe and slice the chestnut mushrooms into similar-sized pieces and add to the wok with the whole button mushrooms. Stir-fry for 3–4 minutes, or until tender. When all the vegetables are tender and the turkey is cooked, add the soy sauce, hoisin sauce, sherry and vegetable stock.

Mix the cornflour with 2 tablespoons of water and add to the wok, then cook, stirring, until the sauce thickens. Add the drained noodles to the wok, then toss the mixture together and serve immediately.

Try this FOR STARTERS: 30 FOR PUDDING: 352

Turkey Tetrazzini

SERVES 4

275 g/10 oz green and white tagliatelle	40 g/1 ½ oz plain flour	freshly grated nutmeg
50 g/2 oz butter	450 ml/¾ pint chicken stock	salt and freshly ground black pepper
4 slices streaky bacon, diced	150 ml/¼ pint double cream	25 g/1 oz Parmesan cheese, grated
1 onion, peeled and finely chopped	2 tbsp sherry	
175 g/6 oz mushrooms, thinly sliced	450 g/1 lb cooked turkey meat, cut into bite-sized pieces	To garnish:
	1 tbsp freshly chopped parsley	freshly chopped parsley
		Parmesan cheese, grated

Preheat the oven to 180°C/350°F/Gas Mark 4. Lightly oil a large ovenproof dish. Bring a large saucepan of lightly salted water to the boil. Add the tagliatelle and cook for 7–9 minutes, or until 'al dente'. Drain well and reserve.

In a heavy-based saucepan, heat the butter and add the bacon. Cook for 2–3 minutes, or until crisp and golden. Add the onion and mushrooms and cook for 3–4 minutes, or until the vegetables are tender.

Stir in the flour and cook for 2 minutes. Remove from the heat and slowly stir in the stock. Return to the heat and cook, stirring until a smooth, thick sauce has formed. Add the tagliatelle, then pour in the cream and sherry. Add the turkey and parsley. Season to taste with the nutmeg and salt and pepper. Toss well to coat.

Turn the mixture into the prepared dish, spreading evenly. Sprinkle the top with the Parmesan cheese and bake in the preheated oven for 30–35 minutes, or until crisp, golden and bubbling. Garnish with chopped parsley and Parmesan cheese. Serve straight from the dish.

Try this: FOR STARTERS: 20   FOR PUDDING: 366

Creamy Turkey & Tomato Pasta

SERVES 4

4 tbsp olive oil
450 g/1 lb turkey breasts,
    cut into bite-sized pieces
550 g/1¼ lb cherry tomatoes,
    on the vine

2 garlic cloves, peeled
    and chopped
4 tbsp balsamic vinegar
4 tbsp freshly chopped basil
salt and freshly ground

black pepper
200 ml tub crème fraîche
350 g/12 oz tagliatelle
shaved Parmesan cheese,
    to garnish

Preheat the oven to 200°C/400°F/Gas Mark 6. Heat 2 tablespoons of the olive oil in a large frying pan. Add the turkey and cook for 5 minutes, or until sealed, turning occasionally. Transfer to a roasting tin and add the remaining olive oil, the vine tomatoes, garlic and balsamic vinegar. Stir well and season to taste with salt and pepper. Cook in the preheated oven for 30 minutes, or until the turkey is tender, turning the tomatoes and turkey once.

Meanwhile, bring a large pan of lightly salted water to a rolling boil. Add the pasta and cook according to the packet instructions, or until 'al dente'. Drain, return to the pan and keep warm. Stir the basil and seasoning into the crème fraîche.

Remove the roasting tin from the oven and discard the vines. Stir the crème fraîche and basil mix into the turkey and tomato mixture and return to the oven for 1–2 minutes, or until thoroughly heated through.

Stir the turkey and tomato mixture into the pasta and toss lightly together. Tip into a warmed serving dish. Garnish with Parmesan cheese shavings and serve immediately.

Try this: FOR STARTERS: 54 FOR PUDDING: 350

Turkey & Oven–roasted Vegetable Salad

SERVES 4

6 tbsp olive oil
3 medium courgettes, trimmed and sliced
2 yellow peppers, deseeded and sliced
125 g/4 oz pine nuts
275 g/10 oz macaroni

350 g/12 oz cooked turkey
280 g jar or can chargrilled artichokes, drained and sliced
225 g/8 oz baby plum tomatoes, quartered
4 tbsp freshly

chopped coriander
1 garlic clove, peeled and chopped
3 tbsp balsamic vinegar
salt and freshly ground black pepper

Preheat the oven to 200°C/400°F/Gas Mark 6, 15 minutes before cooking. Line a large roasting tin with tinfoil, pour in half the olive oil and place in the oven for 3 minutes, or until very hot. Remove from the oven, add the courgettes and peppers and stir until evenly coated. Bake for 30–35 minutes, or until slightly charred, turning occasionally.

Add the pine nuts to the tin. Return to the oven and bake for 10 minutes, or until the pine nuts are toasted. Remove from the oven and allow the vegetables to cool completely.

Bring a large pan of lightly salted water to a rolling boil. Add the macaroni and cook according to the packet instructions, or until 'al dente'. Drain and refresh under cold running water then drain thoroughly and place in a large salad bowl.

Cut the turkey into bite-sized pieces and add to the macaroni. Add the artichokes and tomatoes with the cooled vegetables and pan juices to the pan. Blend together the coriander, garlic, remaining oil, vinegar and seasoning. Pour over the salad, toss lightly and serve.

Turkey with Oriental Mushrooms

SERVES 4

15 g/½ oz dried
  Chinese mushrooms
450 g/1 lb turkey
  breast steaks
150 ml/¼ pint turkey
  or chicken stock
2 tbsp groundnut oil
1 red pepper, deseeded
and sliced
225 g/8 oz sugar snap peas,
  trimmed
125 g/4 oz shiitake
  mushrooms, wiped
  and halved
125 g/4 oz oyster
  mushrooms, wiped
and halved
2 tbsp yellow bean sauce
2 tbsp soy sauce
1 tbsp hot chilli sauce
freshly cooked noodles,
  to serve

Place the dried mushrooms in a small bowl, cover with almost boiling water and leave for 20–30 minutes. Drain and discard any woody stems from the mushrooms. Cut the turkey and into thin strips.

Pour the turkey or chicken stock into a wok or large frying pan and bring to the boil. Add the turkey and cook gently for 3 minutes, or until the turkey is sealed completely, then using a slotted spoon, remove from the wok and reserve. Discard any stock.

Wipe the wok clean and reheat, then add the oil. When the oil is almost smoking, add the drained turkey and stir-fry for 2 minutes.

Add the drained mushrooms to the wok with the red pepper, the sugar snap peas and the shiitake and oyster mushrooms. Stir-fry for 2 minutes, then add the yellow bean, soy and hot chilli sauces.

Stir-fry the mixture for 1–2 minutes more, or until the turkey is cooked thoroughly and the vegetables are cooked but still retain a bite. Turn into a warmed serving dish and serve immediately with freshly cooked noodles.

Try this: FOR STARTERS: 48 FOR PUDDING: 374

Spaghetti with Turkey & Bacon Sauce

SERVES 4

450 g/1 lb spaghetti
25 g /1 oz butter
225 g/8 oz smoked streaky
  bacon, rind removed
350 g/12 oz fresh
  turkey strips

1 onion, peeled
  and chopped
1 garlic clove, peeled and
  chopped
3 medium eggs, beaten
300 ml/½ pint double cream

salt and freshly ground
  black pepper
50 g/2 oz freshly grated
  Parmesan cheese
2–3 tbsp freshly chopped
  coriander, to garnish

Bring a large pan of lightly salted water to a rolling boil. Add the spaghetti and cook according to the packet instructions, or until 'al dente'.

Meanwhile, melt the butter in a large frying pan. Using a sharp knife, cut the streaky bacon into small dice. Add the bacon to the pan with the turkey strips and cook for 8 minutes, or until browned, stirring occasionally to prevent sticking. Add the onion and garlic and cook for 5 minutes, or until softened, stirring occasionally.

Place the eggs and cream in a bowl and season to taste with salt and pepper. Beat together then pour into the frying pan and cook, stirring, for 2 minutes or until the mixture begins to thicken but does not scramble.

Drain the spaghetti thoroughly and return to the pan. Pour over the sauce, add the grated Parmesan cheese and toss lightly. Heat through for 2 minutes, or until piping hot. Tip into a warmed serving dish and sprinkle with freshly chopped coriander. Serve immediately.

Try this: FOR STARTERS: 40   FOR PUDDING: 360

Vegetarian

Pad Thai Noodles with Mushrooms

SERVES 4

125 g/4 oz flat rice noodles or rice vermicelli
1 tbsp vegetable oil
2 garlic cloves, peeled and finely chopped
1 medium egg, lightly beaten
225 g/8 oz mixed

mushrooms, including shiitake, oyster, field, brown and wild mushrooms
2 tbsp lemon juice
1½ tbsp Thai fish sauce
½ tsp sugar
½ tsp cayenne pepper

2 spring onions, trimmed and cut into 2.5 cm/ 1 inch pieces
50 g/2 oz fresh beansprouts

To garnish:
chopped roasted peanuts
freshly chopped coriander

Cook the noodles according to the packet instructions. Drain well and reserve.

Heat a wok or large frying pan. Add the oil and garlic. Fry until just golden. Add the egg and stir quickly to break it up.

Cook for a few seconds before adding the noodles and mushrooms. Scrape down the sides of the pan to ensure they mix with the egg and garlic.

Add the lemon juice, fish sauce, sugar, cayenne pepper, spring onions and half of the beansprouts, stirring quickly all the time.

Cook over a high heat for a further 2–3 minutes until everything is heated through.

Turn on to a serving plate. Top with the remaining beansprouts. Garnish with the chopped peanuts and coriander and serve immediately.

Try this: FOR STARTERS: 36   FOR PUDDING: 380

Baby Onion Risotto

SERVES 4

For the baby onions:
1 tbsp olive oil
450 g/1 lb baby onions,
    peeled and halved if large
pinch of sugar
1 tbsp freshly
    chopped thyme

For the risotto:
1 tbsp olive oil
1 small onion, peeled
    and finely chopped
2 garlic cloves, peeled
    and finely chopped
350 g/12 oz risotto rice
150 ml/¼ pint red wine

1 litre/1 ¾ pint hot
    vegetable stock
125 g/4 oz low-fat soft
    goat's cheese
salt and freshly ground
    black pepper
sprigs of fresh thyme,
    to garnish

For the baby onions, heat the olive oil in a saucepan and add the onions with the sugar. Cover and cook over a low heat, stirring occasionally, for 20–25 minutes until caramelised. Uncover during the last 10 minutes of cooking.

Meanwhile, for the risotto, heat the oil in a large frying pan and add the onion. Cook over a medium heat for 5 minutes until softened. Add the garlic and cook for a further 30 seconds.

Add the risotto rice and stir well. Add the red wine and stir constantly until the wine is almost completely absorbed by the rice. Begin adding the stock a ladleful at a time, stirring well and waiting until the last ladleful has been absorbed before stirring in the next. It will take 20–25 minutes to add all the stock by which time the rice should be just cooked but still firm. Remove from the heat.

Add the thyme to the onions and cook briefly. Increase the heat and allow the onion mixture to bubble for 2–3 minutes until almost evaporated. Add the onion mixture to the risotto along with the goat's cheese. Stir well and season to taste with salt and pepper. Garnish with sprigs of fresh thyme and serve immediately.

Try this: FOR STARTERS: 54   FOR PUDDING: 350

Hot & Spicy Red Cabbage with Apples

SERVES 8

900 g/2 lb red cabbage, cored and shredded	½ tsp mixed spice	50 ml/2 fl oz medium sweet cider (or apple juice)
450 g/1 lb onions, peeled and finely sliced	1 tsp ground cinnamon	2 tbsp wine vinegar
450 g/1 lb cooking apples, peeled, cored and finely sliced	2 tbsp light soft brown sugar	
	salt and freshly ground black pepper	To serve:
	grated rind of 1 large orange	half-fat crème fraîche
	1 tbsp fresh orange juice	freshly ground black pepper

Preheat the oven to 150°C/300°F/Gas Mark 2. Put just enough cabbage in a large casserole dish to cover the base evenly.

Place a layer of the onions and apples on top of the cabbage.

Sprinkle a little of the mixed spice, cinnamon and sugar over the top. Season with salt and pepper.

Spoon over a small portion of the orange rind, orange juice and the cider.

Continue to layer the casserole dish with the ingredients in the same order until used up.

Pour the vinegar as evenly as possible over the top layer of the ingredients.

Cover the casserole dish with a close-fitting lid and bake in the preheated oven, stirring occasionally, for 2 hours until the cabbage is moist and tender. Serve immediately with the crème fraîche and black pepper.

Carrot, Celeriac & Sesame Seed Salad

SERVES 6

225 g/8 oz celeriac
225 g/8 oz carrots, peeled
50 g/2 oz seedless raisins
2 tbsp sesame seeds
freshly chopped parsley,
  to garnish

For the lemon &
  chilli dressing:
grated rind of 1 lemon
4 tbsp lemon juice
2 tbsp sunflower oil
2 tbsp clear honey

1 red bird's eye
  chilli, deseeded and
  finely chopped
salt and freshly ground
  black pepper

Slice the celeriac into thin matchsticks. Place in a small saucepan of boiling salted water and boil for 2 minutes.

Drain and rinse the celeriac in cold water and place in a mixing bowl.

Finely grate the carrot. Add the carrot and the raisins to the celeriac in the bowl.

Place the sesame seeds under a hot grill or dry-fry in a frying pan for 1–2 minutes until golden brown, then leave to cool.

Make the dressing by whisking together the lemon rind, lemon juice, oil, honey, chilli and seasoning or by shaking thoroughly in a screw-topped jar.

Pour 2 tablespoons of the dressing over the salad and toss well. Turn into a serving dish and sprinkle over the toasted sesame seeds and chopped parsley. Serve the remaining dressing separately.

Try this: FOR STARTERS: 64   FOR PUDDING: 362

Vegetarian Cassoulet

SERVES 4

225 g/8 oz dried haricot
    beans, soaked overnight
2 medium onions
1 bay leaf
1.4 litres/2½ pints cold water
550 g/1¼ lb large potatoes,
    peeled and cut into
    1 cm/ ½ inch slices
salt and freshly ground

black pepper
5 tsp olive oil
1 large garlic clove,
    peeled and crushed
2 leeks, trimmed and sliced
200 g can chopped tomatoes
1 tsp dark muscovado sugar
1 tbsp freshly chopped thyme
2 tbsp freshly

chopped parsley
3 courgettes, trimmed
    and sliced

For the topping:
50 g/2 oz fresh white
    breadcrumbs
25 g/1oz Cheddar cheese,
    finely grated

Preheat the oven to 180˚C/350˚F/Gas Mark 4, 10 minutes before required. Drain the beans, rinse under cold running water and put in a saucepan. Peel 1 of the onions and add to the beans with the bay leaf. Pour in the water. Bring to a rapid boil and cook for 10 minutes, then turn down the heat, cover and simmer for 50 minutes, or until the beans are almost tender. Drain the beans, reserving the liquor, but discarding the onion and bay leaf.

Cook the potatoes in a saucepan of lightly salted boiling water for 6–7 minutes until almost tender when tested with the point of a knife. Drain and reserve.

Peel and chop the remaining onion. Heat the oil in a frying pan and cook the onion with the garlic and leeks for 10 minutes until softened. Stir in the tomatoes, sugar, thyme and parsley. Stir in the beans, with 300 ml/½ pint of the reserved liquor and season to taste. Simmer, uncovered, for 5 minutes.Layer the potato slices, courgettes and ladlefuls of the bean mixture in a large flameproof casserole dish. To make the topping, mix together the breadcrumbs and cheese and sprinkle over the top.

Bake in the preheated oven for 40 minutes, or until the vegetables are cooked through and the topping is golden brown and crisp. Serve immediately.

Layered Cheese & Herb Potato Cake

SERVES 4

900 g/2 lb waxy potatoes
3 tbsp freshly snipped chives
2 tbsp freshly
    chopped parsley
225 g/8 oz mature
    Cheddar cheese

2 large egg yolks
1 tsp paprika
125 g/4 oz fresh white
    breadcrumbs

50 g/2 oz almonds, toasted

and roughly chopped
50 g/2 oz butter, melted
salt and freshly ground
    black pepper
mixed salad or steamed
    vegetables, to serve

Preheat the oven to 180˚C/350˚F/Gas Mark 4. Lightly oil and line the base of a 20.5 cm/ 8 inch round cake tin with lightly oiled greaseproof or baking parchment paper. Peel and thinly slice the potatoes and reserve. Stir the chives, parsley, cheese and egg yolks together in a small bowl and reserve. Mix the paprika into the breadcrumbs.

Sprinkle the almonds over the base of the lined tin. Cover with half the potatoes, arranging them in layers, then sprinkle with the paprika breadcrumb mixture and season to taste with salt and pepper.

Spoon the cheese and herb mixture over the breadcrumbs with a little more seasoning, then arrange the remaining potatoes on top. Drizzle over the melted butter and press the surface down firmly.

Bake in the preheated oven for 1¼ hours, or until golden and cooked through. Let the tin stand for 10 minutes before carefully turning out and serving in thick wedges. Serve immediately with salad or freshly cooked vegetables.

Pasta with Raw Fennel, Tomato & Red Onions

SERVES 6

1 fennel bulb
700 g/1½ lb tomatoes
1 garlic clove
¼ small red onion
small handful fresh basil

small handful fresh mint
100 ml/3½ fl oz extra
   virgin olive oil,
   plus extra to serve
juice of 1 lemon

salt and freshly ground
   black pepper
450 g/1 lb penne or pennette
freshly grated Parmesan
   cheese, to serve

Trim the fennel and slice thinly. Stack the slices and cut into sticks, then cut crosswise again into fine dice. Deseed the tomatoes and chop them finely. Peel and finely chop or crush the garlic. Peel and finely chop or grate the onion.

Stack the basil leaves then roll up tightly. Slice crosswise into fine shreds. Finely chop the mint.

Place the chopped vegetables and herbs in a medium bowl. Add the olive oil and lemon juice and mix together. Season well with salt and pepper then leave for 30 minutes to allow the flavours to develop.

Bring a large pan of salted water to a rolling boil. Add the pasta and cook according to the packet instructions, or until 'al dente'.

Drain the cooked pasta thoroughly. Transfer to a warmed serving dish, pour over the vegetable mixture and toss. Serve with the grated Parmesan cheese and extra olive oil to drizzle over.

Try this: FOR STARTERS: 50   FOR PUDDING: 380

Pasta with Walnut Sauce

SERVES 4

50 g/2 oz walnuts, toasted
3 spring onions,
   trimmed and chopped
2 garlic cloves, peeled
   and sliced

1 tbsp freshly chopped
   parsley or basil
5 tbsp extra virgin olive oil
salt and freshly ground
   black pepper

450 g/1 lb broccoli,
   cut into florets
350 g/12 oz pasta shapes
1 red chilli, deseeded and
   finely chopped

Place the toasted walnuts in a blender or food processor with the chopped spring onions, one of the garlic cloves and parsley or basil. Blend to a fairly smooth paste, then gradually add 3 tablespoons of the olive oil, until it is well mixed into the paste. Season the walnut paste to taste with salt and pepper and reserve.

Bring a large pan of lightly salted water to a rolling boil. Add the broccoli, return to the boil and cook for 2 minutes. Remove the broccoli, using a slotted draining spoon and refresh under cold running water. Drain again and pat dry on absorbent kitchen paper.

Bring the water back to a rolling boil. Add the pasta and cook according to the packet instructions, or until 'al dente'.

Meanwhile, heat the remaining oil in a frying pan. Add the remaining garlic and chilli. Cook gently for 2 minutes, or until softened. Add the broccoli and walnut paste. Cook for a further 3–4 minutes, or until heated through.

Drain the pasta thoroughly and transfer to a large warmed serving bowl. Pour over the walnut and broccoli sauce. Toss together, adjust the seasoning and serve immediately.

Try this: FOR STARTERS: 32   FOR PUDDING: 356

Melanzane Parmigiana

SERVES 4

900 g/2 lb aubergines
salt and freshly ground
    black pepper
5 tbsp olive oil
1 red onion,
    peeled and chopped
½ tsp mild paprika pepper

150 ml/¼ pint dry red wine
150 ml/¼ pint
    vegetable stock
400 g can chopped tomatoes
1 tsp tomato purée
1 tbsp freshly
    chopped oregano

175 g/6 oz mozzarella
    cheese, thinly sliced
40 g/11⁄2 oz Parmesan
    cheese, coarsely grated
sprig of fresh basil,
    to garnish

Preheat the oven to 200°C/400°F/Gas Mark 6, 15 minutes before cooking. Cut the aubergines lengthways into thin slices. Sprinkle with salt and leave to drain in a colander over a bowl for 30 minutes.

Meanwhile, heat 1 tablespoon of the olive oil in a saucepan and fry the onion for 10 minutes, until softened. Add the paprika and cook for 1 minute. Stir in the wine, stock, tomatoes and tomato purée. Simmer, uncovered, for 25 minutes, or until fairly thick. Stir in the oregano and season to taste with salt and pepper. Remove from the heat.

Rinse the aubergine slices thoroughly under cold water and pat dry on absorbent kitchen paper. Heat 2 tablespoons of the oil in a griddle pan and cook the aubergines in batches, for 3 minutes on each side, until golden. Drain well on absorbent kitchen paper.

Pour half of the tomato sauce into the base of a large ovenproof dish. Cover with half the aubergine slices, then top with the mozzarella. Cover with the remaining aubergine slices and pour over the remaining tomato sauce. Sprinkle with the grated Parmesan cheese.

Bake in the preheated oven for 30 minutes, or until the aubergines are tender and the sauce is bubbling. Garnish with a sprig of fresh basil and cool for a few minutes before serving.

Rigatoni with Oven–dried Cherry Tomatoes & Mascarpone

SERVES 4

350 g/12 oz red
   cherry tomatoes
1 tsp caster sugar
salt and freshly ground
   black pepper

2 tbsp olive oil
400 g/14 oz dried rigatoni
125 g/4 oz petits pois
2 tbsp mascarpone cheese
1 tbsp freshly chopped mint

1 tbsp freshly
   chopped parsley
sprigs of fresh mint,
   to garnish

Preheat the oven to 140°C/275°F/Gas Mark 1. Halve the cherry tomatoes and place close together on a non-stick baking tray, cut-side up. Sprinkle lightly with the sugar, then with a little salt and pepper. Bake in the preheated oven for 1¼ hours, or until dry, but not beginning to colour. Leave to cool on the baking tray. Put in a bowl, drizzle over the olive oil and toss to coat.

Bring a large saucepan of lightly salted water to the boil and cook the pasta for about 10 minutes or until 'al dente'. Add the petits pois, 2–3 minutes before the end of the cooking time. Drain thoroughly and return the pasta and the petits pois to the saucepan.

Add the mascarpone to the saucepan. When melted, add the tomatoes, mint, parsley and a little black pepper. Toss gently together, then transfer to a warmed serving dish or individual plates and garnish with sprigs of fresh mint. Serve immediately.

Try this: FOR STARTERS: 54 FOR PUDDING: 350

Spaghetti with Pesto

SERVES 4

200 g/7 oz freshly grated
  Parmesan cheese,
  plus extra to serve
25 g/1 oz fresh basil leaves,
  plus extra to garnish

6 tbsp pine nuts
3 large garlic cloves, peeled
200 ml/7 fl oz extra virgin
  olive oil, plus more
  if necessary

salt and freshly
  ground pepper
400 g/14 oz spaghetti

To make the pesto, place the Parmesan cheese in a food processor with the basil leaves, pine nuts and garlic and process until well blended.

With the motor running, gradually pour in the extra virgin olive oil, until a thick sauce forms. Add a little more oil if the sauce seems too thick. Season to taste with salt and pepper. Transfer to a bowl, cover and store in the refrigerator until required.

Bring a large pan of lightly salted water to a rolling boil. Add the spaghetti and cook according to the packet instructions, or until 'al dente'.

Drain the spaghetti thoroughly and return to the pan. Stir in the pesto and toss lightly. Heat through gently, then tip the pasta into a warmed serving dish or spoon on to individual plates. Garnish with basil leaves and serve immediately with extra Parmesan cheese.

Try this: FOR STARTERS: 36   FOR PUDDING: 376

Pasta Shells with Broccoli & Capers

SERVES 4

400 g/14 oz conchiglie (shells)
450 g/1 lb broccoli florets,
    cut into small pieces
5 tbsp olive oil
1 large onion, peeled
    and finely chopped
4 tbsp capers in brine,

rinsed and drained
½ tsp dried chilli flakes
    (optional)
75 g/3 oz freshly grated
    Parmesan cheese,
    plus extra
    to serve

25 g/1 oz pecorino
    cheese, grated
salt and freshly ground
    black pepper
2 tbsp freshly chopped
    flat-leaf parsley,
    to garnish

Bring a large pan of lightly salted water to a rolling boil. Add the orecchiette, return to the boil and cook for 2 minutes. Add the broccoli to the pan. Return to the boil and continue cooking for 8–10 minutes, or until the conchiglie is 'al dente'.

Meanwhile, heat the olive oil in a large frying pan, add the onion and cook for 5 minutes, or until softened, stirring frequently. Stir in the capers and chilli flakes, if using, and cook for a further 2 minutes.

Drain the pasta and broccoli and add to the frying pan. Toss the ingredients to mix thoroughly. Sprinkle over the cheeses, then stir until the cheeses have just melted. Season to taste with salt and pepper, then tip into a warmed serving dish. Garnish with chopped parsley and serve immediately with extra Parmesan cheese.

Try this: FOR STARTERS: 52   FOR PUDDING: 358

Venetian Herb Orzo

SERVES 4-6

200 g/7 oz baby
   spinach leaves
150 g/5 oz rocket leaves
50 g/2 oz flat-leaf parsley

6 spring onions, trimmed
few leaves of fresh mint
3 tbsp extra virgin olive oil,
   plus more if required

450 g/11 oz orzo
salt and freshly ground
   black pepper

Rinse the spinach leaves in several changes of cold water and reserve. Finely chop the rocket leaves with the parsley and mint. Thinly slice the green of the spring onions.

Bring a large saucepan of water to the boil, add the spinach leaves, herbs and spring onions and cook for about 10 seconds. Remove and rinse under cold running water. Drain well and, using your hands, squeeze out all the excess moisture.

Place the spinach, herbs and spring onions in a food processor. Blend for 1 minute then, with the motor running, gradually pour in the olive oil until the sauce is well blended.

Meanwhile, bring a large pan of lightly salted water to a rolling boil. Add the pasta and cook according to the packet instructions, or until 'al dente'. Drain thoroughly and place in a large warmed bowl.

Add the spinach sauce to the orzo and stir lightly until the orzo is well coated. Stir in an extra tablespoon of olive oil if the mixture seems too thick. Season well with salt and pepper. Serve immediately on warmed plates or allow to cool to room temperature.

Try this: FOR STARTERS: 56   FOR PUDDING: 352

Fusilli with Courgettes & Sun-dried Tomatoes

SERVES 6

5 tbsp olive oil
1 large onion, peeled
  and thinly sliced
2 garlic cloves, peeled
  and finely chopped
700 g/1½ lb courgettes,
  trimmed and sliced

400 g can chopped
  plum tomatoes
12 sun-dried tomatoes,
  cut into thin strips
salt and freshly ground
  black pepper
450 g/1 lb fusilli

25 g/1 oz butter, diced
2 tbsp freshly chopped basil
  or flat-leaf parsley
grated Parmesan or
  pecorino cheese,
  for serving

Heat 2 tablespoons of the olive oil in a large frying pan, add the onion and cook for 5-7 minutes, or until softened. Add the chopped garlic and courgette slices and cook for a further 5 minutes, stirring occasionally.

Stir the chopped tomatoes and the sun-dried tomatoes into the frying pan and season to taste with salt and pepper. Cook until the courgettes are just tender and the sauce is slightly thickened.

Bring a large pan of lightly salted water to a rolling boil. Add the fusilli and cook according to the packet instructions, or until 'al dente'.

Drain the fusilli thoroughly and return to the pan. Add the butter and remaining oil and toss to coat. Stir the chopped basil or parsley into the courgette mixture and pour over the fusilli. Toss and tip into a warmed serving dish. Serve with grated Parmesan or pecorino cheese.

Four-cheese Tagliatelle

SERVES 4

300 ml/½ pint whipping cream
4 garlic cloves, peeled and lightly bruised
75 g/3 oz fontina cheese, diced
75 g/3 oz Gruyère

cheese, grated
75 g/3 oz mozzarella cheese, preferably, diced
50 g/2 oz Parmesan cheese, grated, plus extra to serve
salt and freshly ground

black pepper
275 g/10 oz fresh green tagliatelle
1–2 tbsp freshly snipped chives
fresh basil leaves, to garnish

Place the whipping cream with the garlic cloves in a medium pan and heat gently until small bubbles begin to form around the edge of the pan. Using a slotted spoon, remove and discard the garlic cloves.

Add all the cheeses to the pan and stir until melted. Season with a little salt and a lot of black pepper. Keep the sauce warm over a low heat, but do not allow to boil.

Meanwhile, bring a large pan of lightly salted water to the boil. Add the taglietelle, return to the boil and cook for 2–3 minutes, or until 'al dente'.

Drain the pasta thoroughly and return to the pan. Pour the sauce over the pasta, add the chives then toss lightly until well coated. Tip into a warmed serving dish or spoon on to individual plates. Garnish with a few basil leaves and serve immediately with extra Parmesan cheese.

Try this: FOR STARTERS: 28 FOR PUDDING: 378

Courgette Lasagne

SERVES 8

2 tbsp olive oil
1 medium onion, peeled
  and finely chopped
225 g/8 oz mushrooms,
  wiped and thinly sliced
3–4 courgettes, trimmed
  and thinly sliced
2 garlic cloves, peeled
  and finely chopped
½ tsp dried thyme
1–2 tbsp freshly chopped
  basil or flat-leaf parsley
salt and freshly ground
  black pepper
1 quantity prepared white
  sauce (see page 148)
350 g/12 oz lasagne
  sheets, cooked
225 g/8 oz mozzarella
  cheese, grated
50 g/2 oz Parmesan cheese,
  grated
400 g can chopped
  tomatoes, drained

Preheat the oven to 200°C/400°F/Gas Mark 6, 15 minutes before cooking. Heat the oil in a large frying pan, add the onion and cook for 3–5 minutes. Add the mushrooms, cook for 2 minutes then add the courgettes and cook for a further 3–4 minutes, or until tender. Stir in the garlic, thyme and basil or parsley and season to taste with salt and pepper. Remove from the heat and reserve.

Spoon one-third of the white sauce on to the base of a lightly oiled large baking dish. Arrange a layer of lasagne over the sauce. Spread half the courgette mixture over the pasta, then sprinkle with some of the mozzarella and some of the Parmesan cheese. Repeat with more white sauce and another layer of lasagne, then cover with half the drained tomatoes.

Cover the tomatoes with lasagne, the remaining courgette mixture, and some mozzarella and Parmesan cheese. Repeat the layers ending with a layer of lasagne sheets, white sauce and the remaining Parmesan cheese. Bake in the preheated oven for 35 minutes, or until golden. Serve immediately.

Spicy Cucumber Stir Fry

SERVES 4

25 g/1 oz black soya
beans, soaked in cold
water, overnight
1½ cucumbers
2 tsp salt

1 tbsp groundnut oil
½ tsp mild chilli powder
4 garlic cloves, peeled
and crushed
5 tbsp vegetable stock

1 tsp sesame oil
1 tbsp freshly
chopped parsley,
to garnish

Rinse the soaked beans thoroughly, then drain. Place in a saucepan, cover with cold water and bring to the boil, skimming off any scum that rises to the surface. Boil for 10 minutes, then reduce the heat and simmer for 1–1½ hours. Drain and reserve.

Peel the cucumbers, slice lengthways and remove the seeds. Cut into 2.5 cm/1 inch slices and place in a colander over a bowl. Sprinkle the salt over the cucumber and leave for 30 minutes. Rinse thoroughly in cold water, drain and pat dry with absorbent kitchen paper.

Heat a wok or large frying pan, add the oil and when hot, add the chilli powder, garlic and black beans and stir-fry for 30 seconds. Add the cucumber and stir-fry for 20 seconds.

Pour the stock into the wok and cook for 3–4 minutes, or until the cucumber is very tender. The liquid will have evaporated at this stage. Remove from the heat and stir in the sesame oil. Turn into a warmed serving dish, garnish with chopped parsley and serve immediately.

Try this: FOR STARTERS: 64 FOR PUDDING: 356

Chinese Egg Fried Rice

SERVES 4

250 g/9 oz long-grain rice
1 tbsp dark sesame oil
2 large eggs
1 tbsp sunflower oil
2 garlic cloves,
   peeled and crushed
2.5 cm/1 inch piece fresh
   root ginger, peeled

and grated
1 carrot, peeled and
   cut into matchsticks
125 g/4 oz mangetout,
   halved
220 g can water chestnuts,
   drained and halved
1 yellow pepper, deseeded

and diced
4 spring onions, trimmed
   and finely shredded
2 tbsp light soy sauce
½ tsp paprika
salt and freshly ground
   black pepper

Bring a saucepan of lightly salted water to the boil, add the rice and cook for 15 minutes or according to the packet instructions. Drain and leave to cool.

Heat a wok or large frying pan and add the sesame oil. Beat the eggs in a small bowl and pour into the hot wok. Using a fork, draw the egg in from the sides of the pan to the centre until it sets, then turn over and cook the other side. When set and golden turn out on to a board. Leave to cool, then cut into very thin strips.

Wipe the wok clean with absorbent kitchen paper, return to the heat and add the sunflower oil. When hot add the garlic and ginger and stir-fry for 30 seconds. Add the remaining vegetables and continue to stir-fry for 3–4 minutes, or until tender but still crisp.

Stir the reserved cooked rice into the wok with the soy sauce and paprika and season to taste with salt and pepper. Fold in the cooked egg strips and heat through. Tip into a warmed serving dish and serve immediately.

Baked Macaroni Cheese

SERVES 8

450 g/1 lb macaroni
75 g/3 oz butter
1 onion, peeled and
    finely chopped
40 g/1½ oz plain flour
1 litre/1¾ pints milk
1–2 dried bay leaves
½ tsp dried thyme

salt and freshly ground
    black pepper
cayenne pepper
freshly grated nutmeg
2 small leeks, trimmed,
    finely chopped, cooked
    and drained
1 tbsp Dijon mustard

400 g/14 oz mature
    Cheddar cheese, grated
2 tbsp dried breadcrumbs
2 tbsp freshly grated
    Parmesan cheese
basil sprig, to garnish

Preheat the oven to 190°C/375°F/Gas Mark 5, 10 minutes before cooking. Bring a large pan of lightly salted water to a rolling boil. Add the macaroni and cook according to the packet instructions, or until 'al dente'. Drain thoroughly and reserve.

Meanwhile, melt 50 g/2 oz of the butter in a large, heavy-based saucepan, add the onion and cook, stirring frequently, for 5–7 minutes, or until softened. Sprinkle in the flour and cook, stirring constantly, for 2 minutes. Remove the pan from the heat, stir in the milk, return to the heat and cook, stirring, until a smooth sauce has formed.

Add the bay leaf and thyme to the sauce and season to taste with salt, pepper, cayenne pepper and freshly grated nutmeg. Simmer for about 15 minutes, stirring frequently, until thickened and smooth.

Remove the sauce from the heat. Add the cooked leeks, mustard and Cheddar cheese and stir until the cheese has melted. Stir in the macaroni then tip into a lightly oiled baking dish.

Sprinkle the breadcrumbs and Parmesan cheese over the macaroni. Dot with the remaining butter, then bake in the preheated oven for 1 hour, or until golden. Garnish with a basil sprig and serve immediately.

Coconut–baked Courgettes

SERVES 4

3 tbsp groundnut oil
1 onion, peeled and
   finely sliced
4 garlic cloves, peeled
   and crushed

½ tsp chilli powder
1 tsp ground coriander
6–8 tbsp desiccated coconut
1 tbsp tomato purée
700 g/1½ lb courgettes,

thinly sliced
freshly chopped parsley,
   to garnish

Preheat the oven to 180°C/350°F/Gas Mark 4, 10 minutes before cooking. Lightly oil a 1.4 litre/2½ pint ovenproof gratin dish. Heat a wok, add the oil and when hot, add the onion and stir-fry for 2–3 minutes or until softened. Add the garlic, chilli powder and coriander and stir-fry for 1–2 minutes.

Pour 300 ml/½ pint cold water into the wok and bring to the boil. Add the coconut and tomato purée and simmer for 3–4 minutes; most of the water will evaporate at this stage. Spoon 4 tablespoons of the spice and coconut mixture into a small bowl and reserve.

Stir the courgettes into the remaining spice and coconut mixture, coating well. Spoon the courgettes into the oiled gratin dish and sprinkle the reserved spice and coconut mixture evenly over the top. Bake, uncovered, in the preheated oven for 15–20 minutes, or until golden. Garnish with chopped parsley and serve immediately.

Mixed Vegetables Stir Fry

SERVES 4

2 tbsp groundnut oil
4 garlic cloves, peeled
 and finely sliced
2.5 cm/1 inch piece fresh
 root ginger, peeled and
 finely sliced
75 g/3 oz broccoli florets
50 g/2 oz mangetout,

trimmed
75 g/3 oz carrots, peeled and
 cut into matchsticks
1 green pepper, deseeded
 and cut into strips
1 red pepper, deseeded and
 cut into strips
1 tbsp soy sauce

1 tbsp hoisin sauce
1 tsp sugar
salt and freshly ground
 black pepper
4 spring onions, trimmed
 and shredded,
 to garnish

Heat a wok, add the oil and when hot, add the garlic and ginger slices and stir-fry for 1 minute.

Add the broccoli florets to the wok, stir-fry for 1 minute, then add the mangetout, carrots and the green and red peppers and stir-fry for a further 3–4 minutes, or until tender but still crisp.

Blend the soy sauce, hoisin sauce and sugar in a small bowl. Stir well, season to taste with salt and pepper and pour into the wok. Transfer the vegetables to a warmed serving dish. Garnish with shredded spring onions and serve immediately.

Try this: FOR STARTERS: 50   FOR PUDDING: 352

Rigatoni with Gorgonzola & Walnuts

SERVES 4

400 g/14 oz rigatoni
50 g/2 oz butter
125 g/4 oz crumbled
  Gorgonzola cheese
2 tbsp brandy, optional
200 ml/7 fl oz whipping

or double cream
75 g/3 oz walnut pieces,
  lightly toasted and
  coarsely chopped
1 tbsp freshly chopped basil
50 g/2 oz freshly grated

Parmesan cheese
salt and freshly ground
  black pepper
To serve:
cherry tomatoes
fresh green salad leaves

Bring a large pan of lightly salted water to a rolling boil. Add the rigatoni and cook according to the packet instructions, or until 'al dente'. Drain the pasta thoroughly, reserve and keep warm.

Melt the butter in a large saucepan or wok over a medium heat. Add the Gorgonzola cheese and stir until just melted. Add the brandy if using and cook for 30 seconds, then pour in the cream and cook for 1–2 minutes, stirring until the sauce is smooth.

Stir in the walnut pieces, basil and half the Parmesan cheese, then add the rigatoni. Season to taste with salt and pepper. Return to the heat, stirring frequently, until heated through. Divide the pasta among 4 warmed pasta bowls, sprinkle with the remaining Parmesan cheese and serve immediately with cherry tomatoes and fresh green salad leaves.

Try this: FOR STARTERS: 56   FOR PUDDING: 374

Basmati Rice with Saffron & Broad Beans

SERVES 4

1 medium egg	black pepper	1 garlic clove, peeled
2 tbsp olive oil	200 g/7 oz basmati rice	and finely chopped
1 tbsp freshly chopped	50 g/2 oz butter	large pinch saffron strands
mixed herbs	1 small onion, peeled	225 g/8 oz shelled broad
salt and freshly ground	and finely chopped	beans, blanched

Beat the egg with 1 teaspoon of olive oil and the herbs. Season lightly with salt and pepper. Heat the remaining teaspoon of olive oil in a wok or small frying wok. Pour half the egg mixture into the pan, tilting it to coat the bottom. Cook gently until set on top. Flip over and cook for a further 30 seconds. Transfer to a plate and repeat, using the remaining mixture, then reserve.

Wash the rice in several changes of water until the water remains relatively clear. Add the drained rice to a large saucepan of boiling salted water and cook for 12–15 minutes until tender. Drain well and reserve.

Heat the butter with the remaining oil in a wok and add the onion and garlic. Cook gently for 3–4 minutes until the onion is softened. Add the saffron and stir well. Add the drained rice and stir before adding the broad beans. Cook for a further 2–3 minutes, or until heated through.

Meanwhile, roll the egg pancakes into cigar shapes then slice crossways into strips. To serve, divide the rice between individual serving bowls and top with the egg strips.

Try this: FOR STARTERS: 58 FOR PUDDING: 358

Chinese Leaves with Sweet & Sour Sauce

SERVES 4

1 head Chinese leaves	2 tbsp brown sugar	3 tbsp sunflower oil
200 g pack pak choi	3 tbsp red wine vinegar	15 g/½ oz butter
1 tbsp cornflour	3 tbsp orange juice	1 tsp salt
1 tbsp soy sauce	2 tbsp tomato purée	2 tbsp toasted sesame seeds

Discard any tough outer leaves and stalks from the Chinese leaves and pak choi and wash well. Drain thoroughly and pat dry with absorbent kitchen paper. Shred the Chinese leaves and pak choi lengthways. Reserve.

In a small bowl, blend the cornflour with 4 tablespoons of water. Add the soy sauce, sugar, vinegar, orange juice and tomato purée and stir until blended thoroughly.

Pour the sauce into a small saucepan and bring to the boil. Simmer gently for 2–3 minutes, or until the sauce is thickened and smooth.

Meanwhile, heat a wok or large frying pan and add the sunflower oil and butter. When melted, add the prepared Chinese leaves and pak choi, sprinkle with the salt and stir-fry for 2 minutes. Reduce the heat and cook gently for a further 1–2 minutes or until tender.

Transfer the Chinese leaves and pak choi to a warmed serving platter and drizzle over the warm sauce. Sprinkle with the toasted sesame seeds and serve immediately.

Try this: FOR STARTERS: 36   FOR PUDDING: 368

Aubergine & Tomato Layer

SERVES 4

2 aubergines, about
   700 g/1½ lb, trimmed
   and thinly sliced
6 tbsp olive oil
1 onion, peeled and
   finely sliced
1 garlic clove, peeled
   and crushed

400 g can chopped tomatoes
50 ml/2 fl oz red wine
½ tsp sugar
salt and freshly ground
   black pepper
50 g/2 oz butter
40 g/1½ oz flour
450 ml/¾ pint milk

225 g/8 oz fresh egg lasagne
2 medium eggs, beaten
200 ml/7 fl oz Greek yogurt
125 g/3 oz mozzarella
   cheese, grated
fresh basil leaves,
   to garnish

Preheat the oven to 190°C/375°F/Gas Mark 5, 10 minutes before cooking. Brush the aubergine slices with 5 tablespoons of the olive oil and place on a baking sheet. Bake in the preheated oven for 20 minutes, or until tender. Remove from the oven and increase the temperature to 200°C/400°F/ Gas Mark 6.

Heat the remaining oil in a heavy-based pan. Add the onion and garlic, cook for 2–3 minutes then add the tomatoes, wine and sugar. Season to taste with salt and pepper, then simmer for 20 minutes.

Melt the butter in another pan. Stir in the flour, cook for 2 minutes, then whisk in the milk. Cook for 2–3 minutes, or until thickened. Season to taste.

Pour a little white sauce into a lightly oiled, 1.7 litre/3 pint baking dish. Cover with a layer of lasagne, spread with tomato sauce, then add some of the aubergines. Cover thinly with white sauce and sprinkle with a little cheese. Continue to layer in this way, finishing with a layer of lasagne.

Beat together the eggs and yogurt. Season, then pour over the lasagne. Sprinkle with the remaining cheese and bake in the preheated oven for 25–30 minutes, or until golden. Garnish with basil leaves and serve.

Baked Macaroni
with Mushrooms & Leeks

SERVES 4

2 tbsp olive oil
1 onion, peeled and
    finely chopped
1 garlic clove, peeled
    and crushed
2 small leeks, trimmed
    and chopped

450 g/1 lb assorted wild
    mushrooms, trimmed
50 ml/2 fl oz white wine
75 g/3 oz butter
150 ml/¼ pint crème fraîche
    or whipping cream
salt and freshly ground

black pepper
75 g/3 oz fresh white
    breadcrumbs
350 g/12 oz short cut
    macaroni
1 tbsp freshly chopped
    parsley, to garnish

Preheat the oven to 220°C/425° F/Gas Mark 7, 15 minutes before cooking. Heat
1 tablespoon of the olive oil in a large frying pan, add the onion and garlic and cook for 2
minutes. Add the leeks, mushrooms and 25 g/1 oz of the butter then cook for 5 minutes. Pour
in the white wine, cook for 2 minutes then stir in the crème fraîche or cream. Season to taste
with salt and pepper.

Meanwhile, bring a large pan of lightly salted water to a rolling boil. Add the macaroni and cook
according to the packet instructions, or until 'al dente'.

Melt 25 g/1 oz of the butter with the remaining oil in a small frying pan. Add the breadcrumbs
and fry until just beginning to turn golden-brown. Drain on absorbent kitchen paper.

Drain the pasta thoroughly, toss in the remaining butter then tip into a lightly oiled,
1.4 litre/2½ pint shallow baking dish. Cover the pasta with the leek and mushroom mixture
then sprinkle with the fried breadcrumbs. Bake in the preheated oven for 5–10 minutes, or
until golden and crisp. Garnish with chopped parsley and serve.

Try this: FOR STARTERS: 64   FOR PUDDING: 376

Bean & Cashew Stir Fry

SERVES 4

3 tbsp sunflower oil
1 onion, peeled and
    finely chopped
1 celery stalk, trimmed
    and chopped
2.5 cm/1 inch piece fresh
    root ginger, peeled
    and grated
2 garlic cloves, peeled
    and crushed

1 red chilli, deseeded
    and finely chopped
175 g/6 oz fine French beans,
    trimmed and halved
175 g/6 oz mangetout, sliced
    diagonally into 3
75 g/3 oz unsalted
    cashew nuts
1 tsp brown sugar
125 ml/4 fl oz

vegetable stock
2 tbsp dry sherry
1 tbsp light soy sauce
1 tsp red wine vinegar
salt and freshly ground
    black pepper
freshly chopped coriander,
    to garnish

Heat a wok or large frying pan, add the oil and when hot, add the onion and celery and stir-fry gently for 3–4 minutes or until softened.

Add the ginger, garlic and chilli to the wok and stir-fry for 30 seconds. Stir in the French beans and mangetout together with the cashew nuts and continue to stir-fry for 1–2 minutes, or until the nuts are golden brown.

Dissolve the sugar in the stock, then blend with the sherry, soy sauce and vinegar. Stir into the bean mixture and bring to the boil. Simmer gently, stirring occasionally for 3–4 minutes, or until the beans and mangetout are tender but still crisp and the sauce has thickened slightly. Season to taste with salt and pepper. Transfer to a warmed serving bowl or spoon on to individual plates. Sprinkle with freshly chopped coriander and serve immediately.

Try this: FOR STARTERS: 48 FOR PUDDING: 370

Rice with Squash & Sage

SERVES 4–6

450 g/1 lb butternut squash
75 g/3 oz unsalted butter
1 small onion, peeled
  and finely chopped
3 garlic cloves, peeled
  and crushed

2 tbsp freshly
  chopped sage
1 litre/1¾ pints
  vegetable stock
450 g/1 lb Arborio rice
50 g/2 oz pine nuts, toasted

25 g/1 oz freshly grated
  Parmesan cheese
freshly snipped chives,
  to garnish
salt and freshly ground
  black pepper

Peel the squash, cut in half lengthways and remove seeds and stringy flesh. Cut remaining flesh into small cubes and reserve.

Heat the wok, add the butter and heat until foaming, then add the onion, garlic and sage and stir-fry for 1 minute.

Add the squash to the wok and stir-fry for a further 10–12 minutes, or until the squash is tender. Remove from the heat.

Meanwhile, bring the vegetable stock to the boil and add the rice. Cook for 8–10 minutes, or until the rice is just tender but still quite wet.

Add the cooked rice to the squash mixture. Stir in the pine nuts and Parmesan, season to taste with salt and pepper. Garnish with snipped chives and serve immediately.

Try this: FOR STARTERS: 58   FOR PUDDING: 372

Thai-style Cauliflower & Potato Curry

SERVES 4

450 g/1 lb new potatoes, peeled and halved or quartered
350 g/12 oz cauliflower florets
3 garlic cloves, peeled and crushed
1 onion, peeled and finely chopped
40 g/1½ oz ground almonds
1 tsp ground coriander
½ tsp ground cumin
½ tsp turmeric
3 tbsp groundnut oil
salt and freshly ground black pepper
50 g/2 oz creamed coconut, broken into small pieces
200 ml/7 fl oz vegetable stock
1 tbsp mango chutney
sprigs of fresh coriander, to garnish
freshly cooked long-grain rice, to serve

Bring a saucepan of lightly salted water to the boil, add the potatoes and cook for 15 minutes or until just tender. Drain and leave to cool. Boil the cauliflower for 2 minutes, then drain and refresh under cold running water. Drain again and reserve.

Meanwhile, blend the garlic, onion, ground almonds and spices with 2 tablespoons of the oil and salt and pepper to taste in a food processor until a smooth paste is formed. Heat a wok, add the remaining oil and when hot, add the spice paste and cook for 3–4 minutes, stirring continuously.

Dissolve the creamed coconut in 6 tablespoons of boiling water and add to the wok. Pour in the stock, cook for 2–3 minutes, then stir in the cooked potatoes and cauliflower.

Stir in the mango chutney and heat through for 3–4 minutes or until piping hot. Tip into a warmed serving dish, garnish with sprigs of fresh coriander and serve immediately with freshly cooked rice.

Spiced Tomato Pilau

SERVES 2–3

225 g/8 oz basmati rice
40 g/1½ oz unsalted butter
4 green cardamom pods
2 star anise
4 whole cloves
10 black peppercorns

5 cm/2 inch piece
  cinnamon stick
1 large red onion, peeled
  and finely sliced
175 g/6 oz canned
  chopped tomatoes

salt and freshly ground
  black pepper
sprigs of fresh coriander,
  to garnish

Wash the rice in several changes of water until the water remains relatively clear. Drain the rice and cover with fresh water. Leave to soak for 30 minutes. Drain well and reserve.

Heat the wok, then melt the butter and add the cardamoms, star anise, cloves, black peppercorns and the cinnamon stick. Cook gently for 30 seconds. Increase the heat and add the onion. Stir-fry for 7–8 minutes until tender and starting to brown. Add the drained rice and cook a further 2–3 minutes.

Sieve the tomatoes and mix with sufficient warm water to make 450 ml/16 fl oz. Pour this int the wok, season to taste with salt and pepper and bring to the boil.

Cover, reduce the heat to very low and cook for 10 minutes. Remove the wok from the heat and leave covered for a further 10 minutes. Do not lift the lid during cooking or resting. Finally uncover and mix well with a fork, heat for 1 minute, then garnish with the sprigs of fresh coriander and serve immediately.

 Try this: FOR STARTERS: 52 FOR PUDDING: 366

Dinner Parties
& Entertaining

Creamy Salmon
with Dill in Filo Baskets

SERVES 4

1 bay leaf
6 black peppercorns
1 large sprig fresh parsley
175 g/6 oz salmon fillet
4 large sheets filo pastry

fine spray of oil
125 g/4 oz baby
   spinach leaves
8 tbsp fromage frais
2 tsp Dijon mustard

2 tbsp freshly chopped dill
salt and freshly ground
   black pepper

Preheat the oven to 200°C/400°F/Gas Mark 6. Place the bay leaf, peppercorns, parsley and salmon in a frying pan and add enough water to barely cover the fish.

Bring to the boil, reduce the heat and poach the fish for 5 minutes until it flakes easily. Remove it from the pan. Reserve.

Spray each sheet of filo pastry lightly with the oil. Scrunch up the pastry to make a nest shape approximately 12.5 cm/5 inches in diameter.

Place on a lightly oiled baking sheet and cook in the preheated oven for 10 minutes until golden and crisp.

Blanch the spinach in a pan of lightly salted boiling water for 2 minutes. Drain thoroughly and keep warm.

Mix the fromage frais, mustard and dill together, then warm gently. Season to taste with salt and pepper. Divide the spinach between the filo pastry nests and flake the salmon on to the spinach.

Spoon the mustard and dill sauce over the filo baskets and serve immediately.

Try this: FOR STARTERS: 26   FOR PUDDING: 358

Fish Puff Tart

SERVES 4

350 g/12 oz prepared puff
    pastry, thawed if frozen
150 g/5 oz smoked haddock
150 g/5 oz cod

1 tbsp pesto sauce
2 tomatoes, sliced
125 g/4 oz goats'
    cheese, sliced

1 medium egg, beaten
freshly chopped parsley,
    to garnish

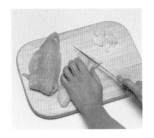

Preheat the oven to 220°C/425°F/Gas Mark 7. On a lightly floured surface roll out the pastry into a 20.5 x 25.5 cm/8 x 10 inch rectangle.

Draw a 18 x 23 cm/7 x 9 inch rectangle in the centre of the pastry, to form a 2.5 cm/1 inch border. Be careful not to cut through the pastry.

Lightly cut criss-cross patterns in the border of the pastry with a knife.

Place the fish on a chopping board and with a sharp knife skin the cod and smoked haddock. Cut into thin slices.

Spread the pesto evenly over the bottom of the pastry case with the back of a spoon.

Arrange the fish, tomatoes and cheese in the pastry case and brush the pastry with the beaten egg.

Bake the tart in the preheated oven for 20–25 minutes, until the pastry is well risen, puffed and golden brown. Garnish with the chopped parsley and serve immediately.

Mussels with Creamy Garlic & Saffron Sauce

SERVES 4

700 g/1½ lb fresh
live mussels
300 ml/½ pint good-quality
dry white wine
1 tbsp olive oil
1 shallot, peeled and

finely chopped
2 garlic cloves, peeled
and crushed
1 tbsp freshly
chopped oregano
2 saffron strands

150 ml/¼ pint single cream
salt and freshly ground
black pepper
fresh crusty bread,
to serve

Clean the mussels thoroughly in plenty of cold water and remove any beards and barnacles from the shells. Discard any mussels that are open or damaged. Place in a large bowl and cover with cold water and leave in the refrigerator until required, if prepared earlier.

Pour the wine into a large saucepan and bring to the boil. Tip the mussels into the pan, cover and cook, shaking the saucepan periodically for 6–8 minutes, or until the mussels have opened completely.

Discard any mussels with closed shells, then using a slotted spoon, carefully remove the remaining open mussels from the saucepan and keep them warm. Reserve the cooking liquor.

Heat the olive oil in a small frying pan and cook the shallot and garlic gently for 2–3 minutes, until softened. Add the reserved cooking liquid and chopped oregano and cook for a further 3–4 minutes. Stir in the saffron and the cream and heat through gently. Season to taste with salt and pepper. Place a few mussels in individual serving bowls and spoon over the saffron sauce. Serve immediately with plenty of fresh crusty bread.

Try this: FOR STARTERS: 18   FOR PUDDING: 350

Parmesan & Garlic Lobster

SERVES 2

1 large cooked lobster	1 tbsp plain flour	sea salt and freshly ground
25 g/1 oz unsalted butter	300 ml/½ pint milk	black pepper
4 garlic cloves, peeled	125 g/4 oz Parmesan	assorted salad leaves,
and crushed	cheese, grated	to serve

Preheat the oven to 180°C/350°F/Gas Mark 4, 10 minutes before cooking. Halve the lobster and crack the claws. Remove the gills, green sac behind the head and the black vein running down the body. Place the two lobster halves in a shallow ovenproof dish.

Melt the butter in a small saucepan and gently cook the garlic for 3 minutes, until softened. Add the flour and stir over a medium heat for 1 minute. Draw the saucepan off the heat then gradually stir in the milk, stirring until the sauce thickens. Return to the heat and cook for 2 minutes, stirring throughout until smooth and thickened. Stir in half the cheese and continue to cook for 1 minute, then season to taste with salt and pepper.

Pour the cheese sauce over the lobster halves and sprinkle with the remaining Parmesan cheese. Bake in the preheated oven for 20 minutes, or until heated through and the cheese sauce is golden brown. Serve with assorted salad leaves.

Try this: FOR STARTERS: 50   FOR PUDDING: 370

Roasted Monkfish with Parma Ham

SERVES 4

700 g/1½ lb monkfish tail
sea salt and freshly
    ground black pepper
4 bay leaves
4 slices fontina cheese,
    rind removed

8 slices Parma ham
225 g/8 oz angel hair pasta
50 g/2 oz butter
the zest and juice of 1 lemon
sprigs of fresh coriander,
    to garnish

To serve:
chargrilled courgettes
chargrilled tomatoes

Preheat the oven to 200°C/400°F/Gas Mark 6, 15 minutes before cooking. Discard any skin from the monkfish tail and cut away and discard the central bone. Cut the fish into four equal-sized pieces and season to taste with salt and pepper and lay a bay leaf on each fillet, along with a slice of cheese.

Wrap each fillet with two slices of the Parma ham, so that the fish is covered completely. Tuck the ends of the Parma ham in and secure with a cocktail stick.

Lightly oil a baking sheet and place in the preheated oven for a few minutes. Place the fish on the preheated baking sheet, then place in the oven and cook for 12–15 minutes.

Bring a large saucepan of lightly salted water to the boil, then slowly add the pasta and cook for 5 minutes until 'al dente', or according to packet directions. Drain, reserving 2 tablespoons of the pasta-cooking liquor. Return the pasta to the saucepan and add the reserved pasta liquor, butter, lemon zest and juice. Toss until the pasta is well coated and glistening.

Twirl the pasta into small nests on four warmed serving plates and top with the monkfish parcels. Garnish with sprigs of coriander and serve with chargrilled courgettes and tomatoes.

Pan–fried Salmon with Herb Risotto

SERVES 4

4 x 175 g/6 oz salmon fillets	225 g/8 oz Arborio rice	2 tbsp freshly chopped
3–4 tbsp plain flour	150 ml/¼ pint dry white wine	flat-leaf parsley
1 tsp dried mustard powder	1.4 litres/2½ pints vegetable	knob of butter
salt and freshly ground	or fish stock	
black pepper	50 g/2 oz butter	To garnish:
2 tbsp olive oil	2 tbsp freshly	slices of lemon
3 shallots, peeled	snipped chives	sprigs of fresh dill
and chopped	2 tbsp freshly chopped dill	tomato salad, to serve

Wipe the salmon fillets with a clean, damp cloth. Mix together the flour, mustard powder and seasoning on a large plate and use to coat the salmon fillets and reserve.

Heat half the olive oil in a large frying pan and fry the shallots for 5 minutes until softened, but not coloured. Add the rice and stir for 1 minute, then slowly add the wine, bring to the boil and boil rapidly until reduced by half.

Bring the stock to a gentle simmer, then add to the rice, a ladleful at a time. Cook, stirring frequently, until all the stock has been added and the rice is cooked but still retains a bite. Stir in the butter and freshly chopped herbs and season to taste with salt and pepper.

Heat the remaining olive oil and the knob of butter in a large griddle pan, add the salmon fillets and cook for 2–3 minutes on each side, or until cooked. Arrange the herb risotto on warm serving plates and top with the salmon. Garnish with slices of lemon and sprigs of dill and serve immediately with a tomato salad.

Spaghetti with Smoked Salmon & Tiger Prawns

SERVES 4

225 g/8 oz baby
spinach leaves
salt and freshly ground
black pepper
pinch freshly grated nutmeg
225 g/8 oz cooked
tiger prawns in

their shells, cooked
450 g/1 lb fresh angel
hair spaghetti
50 g/2 oz butter
3 medium eggs
1 tbsp freshly chopped dill,
plus extra to garnish

125 g/4 oz smoked salmon,
cut into strips
dill sprigs,
to garnish
2 tbsp grated
Parmesan cheese,
to serve

Cook the baby spinach leaves in a large pan with 1 teaspoon of water for 3–4 minutes, or until wilted. Drain thoroughly, season to taste with salt, pepper and nutmeg and keep warm. Remove the shells from all but 4 of the tiger prawns and reserve.

Bring a large pan of lightly salted water to a rolling boil. Add the pasta and cook according to the packet instructions, about 3–4 minutes, or until 'al dente'. Drain thoroughly and return to the pan. Stir in the butter and the peeled prawns, cover and keep warm.

Beat the eggs with the dill, season well, then stir into the spaghettini and prawns. Return the pan to the heat briefly, just long enough to lightly scramble the eggs, then remove from the heat. Carefully mix in the smoked salmon strips and the cooked spinach. Toss gently to mix. Tip into a warmed serving dish and garnish with the reserved prawns and dill sprigs. Serve immediately with grated Parmesan cheese.

Thai Coconut Crab Curry

SERVES 4–6

1 onion
4 garlic cloves
5 cm/2 inch piece fresh
   root ginger
2 tbsp vegetable oil
2–3 tsp hot curry paste

400 g/14 oz coconut milk
2 large dressed crabs, white
   and dark meat separated
2 lemon grass stalks, peeled
   and bruised
6 spring onions, trimmed

   and chopped
2 tbsp freshly shredded
   Thai basil or mint,
   plus extra, to garnish
freshly boiled rice,
   to serve

Peel the onion and chop finely. Peel the garlic cloves, then either crush or finely chop.
Peel the ginger and either grate coarsely or cut into very thin shreds. Reserve.

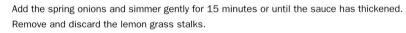

Heat a wok or large frying pan, add the oil and when hot, add the onion, garlic and ginger
and stir-fry for 2 minutes, or until the onion is beginning to soften. Stir in the curry paste and
stir-fry for 1 minute.

Stir the coconut milk into the vegetable mixture with the dark crabmeat. Add the lemon grass,
then bring the mixture slowly to the boil, stirring frequently.

Add the spring onions and simmer gently for 15 minutes or until the sauce has thickened.
Remove and discard the lemon grass stalks.

Add the white crabmeat and the shredded basil or mint and stir very gently for 1–2 minutes
or until heated through and piping hot. Try to prevent the crabmeat from breaking up.

Spoon the curry over boiled rice on warmed individual plates, sprinkle with basil or mint leaves
and serve immediately.

Farfalle with Smoked Trout in a Dill & Vodka Sauce

SERVES 4

400 g/14 oz farfalle	2 tsp wholegrain mustard	black pepper
150 g/5 oz smoked trout	2 tbsp freshly chopped dill	sprigs of dill, to garnish
2 tsp lemon juice	4 tbsp vodka	
200 ml/7 fl oz double cream	salt and freshly ground	

Bring a large pan of lightly salted water to a rolling boil. Add the pasta and cook according to the packet instructions, or until 'al dente'.

Meanwhile, cut the smoked trout into thin slivers, using scissors. Sprinkle lightly with the lemon juice and reserve.

Place the cream, mustard, chopped dill and vodka in a small pan. Season lightly with salt and pepper. Bring the contents of the pan to the boil and simmer gently for 2-3 minutes, or until slightly thickened.

Drain the cooked pasta thoroughly, then return to the pan. Add the smoked trout to the dill and vodka sauce, then pour over the pasta. Toss gently until the pasta is coated and the trout evenly mixed.

Spoon into a warmed serving dish or on to individual plates. Garnish with sprigs of dill and serve immediately.

Seafood Parcels with Pappardelle & Coriander Pesto

SERVES 4

300 g/11 oz pappardelle
  or tagliatelle
8 raw tiger prawns, shelled
12 raw queen scallops
225 g/8oz baby squid,
  cleaned and cut into rings
4 tbsp dry white wine

4 thin slices of lemon

For the coriander pesto:
50 g/2 oz fresh
  coriander leaves
1 garlic clove, peeled
25 g/1 oz pine nuts, toasted

1 tsp lemon juice
5 tbsp olive oil
1 tbsp grated
  Parmesan cheese
salt and freshly ground
  black pepper

Preheat the oven to 180°C/350°F/Gas Mark 4, 10 minutes before cooking. To make the pesto, blend the coriander leaves, garlic, pine nuts and lemon juice with 1 tablespoon of the olive oil to a smooth paste in a food processor. With the motor running slowly add the remaining oil. Stir the Parmesan cheese into the pesto and season to taste with salt and pepper.

Bring a pan of lightly salted water to a rolling boil. Add the pasta and cook for 3 minutes only. Drain thoroughly, return to the pan and spoon over two-thirds of the pesto. Toss to coat.

Cut out four circles, about 30 cm/12 in in diameter, from non-stick baking parchment. Spoon the pasta on to one half of each circle. Top each pile of pasta with 2 prawns, 3 scallops and a few squid rings. Spoon 1 tablespoon of wine over each serving, then drizzle with the remaining coriander pesto and top with a slice of lemon.

Close the parcels by folding over the other half of the paper, to make a semi-circle, then turn and twist the edges of the paper to secure.

Place the parcels on a baking tray and bake in the preheated oven for 15 minutes, or until cooked. Serve the parcels immediately, allowing each person to open their own.

Chinese Steamed Sea Bass
with Black Beans

SERVES 4

1.1 kg/2½ lb sea bass,
   cleaned with head
   and tail left on
1–2 tbsp rice wine
   or dry sherry
1½ tbsp groundnut oil
2–3 tbsp fermented black
   beans, rinsed and drained

1 garlic clove, peeled and
   finely chopped
1 cm/½ inch piece fresh root
   ginger, peeled
   and finely chopped
4 spring onions,
   trimmed and thinly
   sliced diagonally

2–3 tbsp soy sauce
125 ml/4 fl oz fish
   or chicken stock
1–2 tbsp sweet Chinese chilli
   sauce, or to taste
2 tsp sesame oil
sprigs of fresh coriander,
   to garnish

Using a sharp knife, cut 3–4 deep diagonal slashes along both sides of the fish. Sprinkle the Chinese rice wine or sherry inside and over the fish and gently rub into the skin on both sides.

Lightly brush a heatproof plate large enough to fit into a large wok or frying pan with a little of the groundnut oil. Place the fish on the plate, curving the fish along the inside edge of the dish, then leave for 20 minutes.

Place a wire rack or inverted ramekin in the wok and pour in enough water to come about 2.5 cm/1 inch up the side. Bring to the boil over a high heat. Carefully place the plate with the fish on the rack or ramekin, cover and steam for 12–15 minutes, or until the fish is tender and the flesh is opaque when pierced with a knife near the bone.

Remove the plate with the fish from the wok and keep warm. Remove the rack or ramekin from the wok and pour off the water. Return the wok to the heat, add the remaining groundnut oil and swirl to coat the bottom and side. Add the black beans, garlic and ginger and stir-fry for 1 minute

Add the spring onions, soy sauce, fish or chicken stock and boil for 1 minute. Stir in the chilli sauce and sesame oil, then pour the sauce over the cooked fish. Garnish with coriander sprigs and serve immediately.

Try this: FOR STARTERS: 30   FOR PUDDING: 376

Salmon & Spaghetti
in a Creamy Egg Sauce

SERVES 4

3 medium eggs
1 tbsp freshly
   chopped parsley
1 tbsp freshly chopped dill
40 g/1½ oz freshly grated
   Parmesan cheese

40 g/1½ oz freshly grated
   pecorino cheese
2 tbsp dry white wine
freshly ground black pepper
400 g/14 oz spaghetti
350 g/12 oz salmon

fillet, skinned
25 g/1 oz butter
1 tsp olive oil
flat-leaf parsley sprigs,
   to garnish

Beat the eggs in a bowl with the parsley, dill, half of the Parmesan and pecorino cheeses and the white wine. Season to taste with freshly ground black pepper and reserve.

Bring a large pan of lightly salted water to a rolling boil. Add the spaghetti and cook according to the packet instructions, or until 'al dente'.

Meanwhile, cut the salmon into bite-sized pieces. Melt the butter in a large frying pan with the oil and cook the salmon pieces for 3–4 minutes, or until opaque.

Drain the spaghetti thoroughly, return to the pan and immediately add the egg mixture. Remove from the heat and toss well; the eggs will cook in the heat of the spaghetti to make a creamy sauce.

Stir in the remaining cheeses and the cooked pieces of salmon and toss again. Tip into a warmed serving bowl or on to individual plates. Garnish with sprigs of flat-leaf parsley and serve immediately.

Penne with Vodka & Caviar

SERVES 4

400 g/14 oz penne
25 g/1 oz butter
4–6 spring onions, trimmed
  and thinly sliced
1 garlic clove, peeled

and finely chopped
125 ml/4 fl oz vodka
200 ml/7 fl oz double cream
1–2 ripe plum tomatoes,
  skinned, deseeded

and chopped
75 g/3 oz caviar
salt and freshly ground
  black pepper

Bring a large pan of lightly salted water to a rolling boil. Add the penne and cook according to the packet instructions, or until 'al dente'. Drain thoroughly and reserve.

Heat the butter in a large frying pan or wok, add the spring onions and stir-fry for 1 minute. Stir in the garlic and cook for a further 1 minute. Pour the vodka into the pan; it will bubble and steam. Cook until the vodka is reduced by about half, then add the double cream and return to the boil. Simmer gently for 2–3 minutes, or until the sauce has thickened slightly.

Stir in the tomatoes, then stir in all but 1 tablespoon of the caviar and season to taste with salt and pepper. Add the penne and toss lightly to coat. Cook for 1 minute, or until heated through. Divide the mixture among four warmed pasta bowls and garnish with the reserved caviar. Serve immediately.

Try this: FOR STARTERS: 52   FOR PUDDING: 378

Scallops & Prawns Braised in Lemon Grass

SERVES 4-6

450 g/1 lb large raw prawns, peeled with tails left on
350 g/12 oz scallops, with coral attached
2 red chillies, deseeded and coarsely chopped
2 garlic cloves, peeled and coarsely chopped
4 shallots, peeled
1 tbsp shrimp paste
2 tbsp freshly chopped coriander
400 ml/14 fl oz coconut milk
2–3 lemon grass stalks, outer leaves discarded and bruised
2 tbsp Thai fish sauce
1 tbsp sugar
freshly steamed basmati rice, to serve

Rinse the prawns and scallops and pat dry with absorbent kitchen paper. Using a sharp knife, remove the black vein along the back of the prawns. Reserve.

Place the chillies, garlic, shallots, shrimp paste and 1 tablespoon of the chopped coriander in a food processor. Add 1 tablespoon of the coconut milk and 2 tablespoons of water and blend to form a thick paste. Reserve the chilli paste.

Pour the remaining coconut milk with 3 tablespoons of water into a large wok or frying pan, add the lemon grass and bring to the boil. Simmer over a medium heat for 10 minutes or until reduced slightly.

Stir the chilli paste, fish sauce and sugar into the coconut milk and continue to simmer for 2 minutes, stirring occasionally.

Add the prepared prawns and scallops and simmer gently, for 3 minutes, stirring occasionally, or until cooked and the prawns are pink and the scallops are opaque.

Remove the lemon grass and stir in the remaining chopped coriander. Serve immediately spooned over freshly steamed basmati rice.

Try this: FOR STARTERS: 48   FOR PUDDING: 352

Salmon Teriyaki with Noodles & Crispy Greens

SERVES 4

350 g/12 oz salmon fillet
3 tbsp Japanese soy sauce
3 tbsp mirin or sweet sherry
3 tbsp sake
1 tbsp freshly grated
   root ginger

225 g/8 oz spring greens
groundnut oil for deep-frying
pinch of salt
½ tsp caster sugar
125 g/4 oz cellophane
   noodles

To garnish:
1 tbsp freshly chopped dill
sprigs of fresh dill
zest of ½ lemon

Cut the salmon into paper-thin slices and place in a shallow dish. Mix together the soy sauce, mirin or sherry, sake and the ginger. Pour over the salmon, cover and leave to marinate for 15–30 minutes.Remove and discard the thick stalks from the spring greens. Lay several leaves on top of each other, roll up tightly, then shred finely.

Pour in enough oil to cover about 5 cm/2 inches of the wok. Deep-fry the greens in batches for about 1 minute each until crisp. Remove and drain on absorbent kitchen paper. Transfer to a serving dish, sprinkle with salt and sugar and toss together.

Place the noodles in a bowl and pour over warm water to cover. Leave to soak for 15–20 minutes until soft, then drain. With scissors cut into 15 cm/6 inch lengths.

Preheat the grill. Remove the salmon slices from the marinade, reserving the marinade for later, and arrange them in a single layer on a baking sheet. Grill for about 2 minutes, until lightly cooked, without turning.When the oil in the wok is cool enough, tip most of it away, leaving about 1 tablespoon behind. Heat until hot, then add the noodles and the reserved marinade and stir-fry for 3–4 minutes. Tip the noodles into a large warmed serving bowl and arrange the salmon slices on top, garnished with chopped dill, sprigs of fresh dill and lemon zest. Scatter with a little of the crispy greens and serve the rest separately.

Gnocchi & Parma Ham Bake

SERVES 4

3 tbsp olive oil
1 red onion, peeled
    and sliced
2 garlic cloves, peeled
175 g/6 oz plum tomatoes,
    skinned and quartered
2 tbsp sun-dried tomato paste

250 g tub mascarpone cheese
salt and freshly ground
    black pepper
1 tbsp freshly
    chopped tarragon
300 g/11 oz fresh gnocchi
125 g/4 oz Cheddar or

Parmesan cheese, grated
50 g/2 oz fresh white
    breadcrumbs
50 g/2 oz Parma ham, sliced
10 pitted green olives, halved
sprigs of flat-leaf parsley,
    to garnish

Heat the oven to 180° C/350°F/Gas Mark 4, 10 minutes before cooking. Heat 2 tablespoons of the olive oil in a large frying pan and cook the onion and garlic for 5 minutes, or until softened. Stir in the tomatoes, sun-dried tomato paste and mascarpone cheese. Season to taste with salt and pepper. Add half the tarragon. Bring to the boil, then lower the heat immediately and simmer for 5 minutes.

Meanwhile, bring 1.7 litres/3 pints water to the boil in a large pan. Add the remaining olive oil and a good pinch of salt. Add the gnocchi and cook for 1–2 minutes, or until they rise to the surface.

Drain the gnocchi thoroughly and transfer to a large ovenproof dish. Add the tomato sauce and toss gently to coat the pasta. Combine the Cheddar or Parmesan cheese with the breadcrumbs and remaining tarragon and scatter over the pasta mixture. Top with the Parma ham and olives and season again.

Cook in the preheated oven for 20–25 minutes, or until golden and bubbling. Serve immediately, garnished with parsley sprigs.

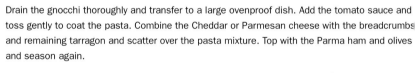

Try this: FOR STARTERS: 24   FOR PUDDING: 374

Pork with Tofu

SERVES 4

450 g/1 lb smoked
    firm tofu, drained
2 tbsp groundnut oil
3 garlic cloves, peeled
    and crushed
2.5 cm/1 inch piece fresh
    root ginger, peeled and

finely chopped
350 g/12 oz fresh pork mince
1 tbsp chilli powder
1 tsp sugar
2 tbsp Chinese rice wine
1 tbsp dark soy sauce
1 tbsp light soy sauce

2 tbsp yellow bean sauce
1 tsp Szechuan peppercorns
75 ml/3 fl oz chicken stock
spring onions, trimmed
    and finely sliced,
    to garnish
fried rice, to serve

Cut the tofu into 1 cm/½ inch cubes and place in a sieve to drain. Place the tofu on absorbent kitchen paper to dry thoroughly for another 10 minutes.

Heat the wok, add the groundnut oil and when hot, add the garlic and ginger. Stir-fry for a few seconds to flavour the oil, but not to colour the vegetables. Add the pork mince and stir-fry for 3 minutes, or until the pork is sealed and there are no lumps in the mince.

Add all the remaining ingredients except for the tofu. Bring the mixture to the boil, then reduce the heat to low. Add the tofu and mix it in gently, taking care not to break up the tofu chunks, but ensuring an even mixture of ingredients. Simmer, uncovered, for 15 minutes, or until the tofu is tender. Turn into a warmed serving dish, garnish with sliced spring onions and serve immediately with fried rice.

Try this: FOR STARTERS: 58   FOR PUDDING: 380

Apple–tossed Pork

SERVES 4

350 g/12 oz pork fillet
2 tbsp plain flour
salt and freshly ground
   black pepper
1½ tbsp sunflower oil

15 g/½ oz unsalted butter
2 dessert apples, peeled,
   cored and thinly sliced
2 tsp Dijon mustard
1 tbsp freshly chopped sage

2 tbsp Calvados brandy
4 tbsp crème fraîche
fresh sage leaves, to garnish
freshly cooked beans,
   to serve

Trim away any visible fat from the pork fillet, then cut across into 1 cm/½ inch thick slices. Season the flour, then add the pork slices a few at a time and toss until lightly coated.

Heat a wok, then add the oil and heat. Stir-fry the meat in two batches over a fairly high heat until well browned. Remove from the wok and reserve.

Melt the butter in the wok, add the apple slices and cook, stirring all the time, for 1 minute. Stir in the mustard, chopped sage, Calvados brandy and crème fraîche. Bring to the boil, stirring.

Return the pork and any juices to the wok and cook over a gentle heat for 1–2 minutes, or until the meat has warmed though, the apples are just tender and the sauce is bubbling. Spoon onto warmed plates, garnish with fresh sage leaves and serve immediately with freshly cooked green beans.

Try this: FOR STARTERS: 40 FOR PUDDING: 362

Lamb with Black Cherry Sauce

SERVES 4

550 g/1¼ lb lamb fillet
2 tbsp light soy sauce
1 tsp Chinese five
  spice powder
4 tbsp fresh orange juice
175 g/6 oz black cherry jam

150 ml/¼ pint red wine
50 g/2 oz fresh
  black cherries
1 tbsp groundnut oil
1 tbsp freshly chopped
  coriander, to garnish

To serve:
thawed frozen peas
freshly cooked noodles

Remove the skin and any fat from the lamb fillet and cut into thin slices. Place in a shallow dish. Mix together the soy sauce, Chinese five spice powder and orange juice and pour over the meat. Cover and leave in the refrigerator for at least 30 minutes.

Meanwhile, blend the jam and the wine together, pour into a small saucepan and bring to the boil. Simmer gently for 10 minutes until slightly thickened. Remove the stones from the cherries, using a cherry stoner if possible in order to keep them whole.

Drain the lamb when ready to cook. Heat the wok, add the oil and when the oil is hot, stir-fry the slices of lamb for 3–5 minutes, or until just slightly pink inside or cooked to personal preference.

Spoon the lamb into a warm serving dish and serve immediately with a little of the cherry sauce drizzled over. Garnish with the chopped coriander and the whole cherries and serve immediately with peas, freshly cooked noodles and the remaining sauce.

Try this: FOR STARTERS: 62   FOR PUDDING: 366

Veal Escalopes with Marsala Sauce

SERVES 6

6 veal escalopes, about
125 g/4 oz each
lemon juice
salt and freshly ground
black pepper
6 sage leaves
6 slices prosciutto

2 tbsp olive oil
25 g/1 oz butter
1 onion, peeled and sliced
1 garlic clove, peeled
and chopped
2 tbsp Marsala wine
4 tbsp double cream

2 tbsp freshly
chopped parsley
sage leaves, to garnish
selection of freshly
cooked vegetables,
to serve

Place the veal escalopes between sheets of non-pvc clingfilm and using a mallet or rolling pin, pound lightly to flatten out thinly to about 5 mm/¼ inch thickness. Remove the clingfilm and sprinkle the veal escalopes with lemon juice, salt and black pepper.

Place a sage leaf in the centre of each escalope. Top with a slice of prosciutto making sure it just fits, then roll up the escalopes enclosing the prosciutto and sage leaves. Secure each escalope with a cocktail stick.

Heat the olive oil and butter in a large non-stick frying pan and fry the onions for 5 minutes, or until softened. Add the garlic and rolled escalopes and cook for about 8 minutes, turning occasionally, until the escalopes are browned all over.

Add the Marsala wine and cream to the pan and bring to the boil, cover and simmer for 10 minutes, or until the veal is tender. Season to taste and then sprinkle with the parsley. Discard the cocktail sticks and serve immediately with a selection of freshly cooked vegetables.

Try this: FOR STARTERS: 64   FOR PUDDING: 372

Fettuccine with Calves' Liver & Calvados

SERVES 4

450 g/1 lb calves' liver, trimmed and thinly sliced	1 tsp paprika	150 ml/¼ pint whipping cream
50 g/2 oz plain flour	50 g/2 oz butter	350 g/12 oz fresh fettuccine
salt and freshly ground black pepper	1½ tbsp olive oil	fresh thyme sprigs, to garnish
	2 tbsp Calvados	
	150 ml/¼ pint cider	

Season the flour with the salt, black pepper and paprika, then toss the liver in the flour until well coated.

Melt half the butter and 1 tablespoon of the olive oil in a large frying pan and fry the liver in batches for 1 minute, or until just browned but still slightly pink inside. Remove using a slotted spoon and place in a warmed dish.

Add the remaining butter to the pan, stir in 1 tablespoon of the seasoned flour and cook for 1 minute. Pour in the Calvados and cider and cook over a high heat for 30 seconds. Stir the cream into the sauce and simmer for 1 minute to thicken slightly, then season to taste. Return the liver to the pan and heat through.

Bring a large pan of lightly salted water to a rolling boil. Add the fettuccine and cook according to the packet instructions, about 3–4 minutes, or until 'al dente'.

Drain the fettuccine thoroughly, return to the pan and toss in the remaining olive oil. Divide among 4 warmed plates and spoon the liver and sauce over the pasta. Garnish with thyme sprigs and serve immediately.

Pan–fried Beef with Creamy Mushrooms

SERVES 4

225 g/8 oz shallots, peeled
2 garlic cloves, peeled
2 tbsp olive oil
4 medallions of beef
4 plum tomatoes

125 g/4 oz flat mushrooms
3 tbsp brandy
150 ml/¼ pint red wine
salt and freshly ground
    black pepper

4 tbsp double cream

To serve:
baby new potatoes
freshly cooked green beans

Cut the shallots in half if large, then chop the garlic. Heat the oil in a large frying pan and cook the shallots for about 8 minutes, stirring occasionally, until almost softened. Add the garlic and beef and cook for 8–10 minutes, turning once during cooking until the meat is browned all over. Using a slotted spoon, transfer the beef to a plate and keep warm.

Rinse the tomatoes and cut into eighths, then wipe the mushrooms and slice. Add to the pan and cook for 5 minutes, stirring frequently until the mushrooms have softened.

Pour in the brandy and heat through. Draw the pan off the heat and carefully ignite. Allow the flames to subside. Pour in the wine, return to the heat and bring to the boil. Boil until reduced by one-third. Draw the pan off the heat, season to taste with salt and pepper, add the cream and stir.

Arrange the beef on serving plates and spoon over the sauce. Serve with baby new potatoes and a few green beans.

Try this: FOR STARTERS: 56   FOR PUDDING: 350

Brandied Beef

SERVES 4

450 g/1 lb rump steak
2 tsp dark soy sauce
1 tsp soft dark brown sugar
salt and freshly ground
   black pepper
1 small fennel bulb

1 red pepper
1 orange
2 tbsp sunflower oil
15 g/½ oz unsalted butter
225 g/8 oz tiny whole
   button mushrooms

5 tbsp beef stock
3 tbsp brandy
orange wedges, to garnish
freshly cooked rice or
   noodles, to serve

Trim any fat from the steak and cut across the grain into thin strips. Place in a shallow bowl with the soy sauce, sugar and a little salt and pepper. Mix well and leave to marinate while preparing the vegetables.

Trim the fennel and slice as thinly as possible, from the stems down through the root. Quarter deseed and thinly slice the red pepper. Thinly pare the rind from about half the orange and cu into fine matchsticks. Squeeze out the juice.

Heat the oil and butter in a wok, add the beef and stir-fry for 2 minutes, until brown and tender Remove with a slotted spoon and reserve.

Add the fennel, red pepper and mushrooms to the wok and stir-fry for 3–4 minutes, or until softened. Add the orange zest and juice and the stock and cook for 2 minutes until the sauce is reduced slightly. Return the beef to the wok and stir-fry for 30 seconds to heat through.

Heat the brandy in a small saucepan or ladel, ignite, then let the flames subside and pour over the vegetables and meat. Gently shake the wok occasionally until the flames subside. Garnish with a few orange wedges and serve immediately with rice or noodles.

Try this: FOR STARTERS: 34 FOR PUDDING: 376

Potato–stuffed Roast Poussin

SERVES 4

4 oven-ready poussins
salt and freshly ground
  black pepper
1 lemon, cut into quarters
450 g/1 lb floury potatoes,
  peeled and cut into
  4 cm/1½ inch pieces

1 tbsp freshly chopped
  thyme or rosemary
3–4 tbsp olive oil
4 garlic cloves, unpeeled
  and lightly smashed
8 slices streaky bacon
  or Parma ham

125 ml/4 fl oz white wine
2 spring onions, trimmed
  and thinly sliced
2 tbsp double cream
  or crème fraîche
lemon wedges,
  to garnish

Preheat the oven to 220°C/425°F/Gas Mark 7. Place a roasting tin in the oven to heat. Rinse the poussin cavities and pat dry with absorbent kitchen paper. Season the cavities with salt and pepper and a squeeze of lemon. Push a lemon quarter into each cavity.

Put the potatoes in a saucepan of lightly salted water and bring to the boil. Reduce the heat to low and simmer until just tender; do not overcook. Drain and cool slightly. Sprinkle the chopped herbs over the potatoes and drizzle with 2–3 tablespoons of the oil. Spoon half the seasoned potatoes into the poussin cavities; do not pack too tightly. Rub each poussin with a little more oil and season with pepper. Carefully spoon 1 tablespoon of oil into the hot roasting tin and arrange the poussins in the tin. Spoon the remaining potatoes around the edge. Sprinkle over the garlic.

Roast the poussins in the preheated oven for 30 minutes, or until the skin is golden and beginning to crisp. Carefully lay the bacon slices over the breast of each poussin and continue to roast for 15–20 minutes until crisp and the poussins are cooked through. Transfer the poussins and potatoes to a serving platter and cover loosely with tinfoil. Skim off the fat from the juices. Place the tin over a medium heat, add the wine and spring onions. Cook briefly, scraping the bits from the bottom of the tin. Whisk in the cream or crème fraîche and bubble for 1 minute, or until thickened. Garnish the poussins with lemon wedges, and serve with the creamy gravy.

Try this: FOR STARTERS: 46   FOR PUDDING: 370

Chicken with Porcini Mushrooms & Cream

SERVES 4

2 tbsp olive oil
4 boneless chicken breasts,
   preferably free range
2 garlic cloves, peeled
   and crushed
150 ml/¼ pint dry vermouth

   or dry white wine
salt and freshly ground
   black pepper
25 g/1 oz butter
450 g/1 lb porcini or wild
   mushrooms, thickly sliced

1 tbsp freshly
   chopped oregano
sprigs of fresh basil,
   to garnish (optional)
freshly cooked rice,
   to serve

Heat the olive oil in a large, heavy-based frying pan, then add the chicken breasts, skin-side down and cook for about 10 minutes, or until they are well browned. Remove the chicken breasts and reserve. Add the garlic, stir into the juices and cook for 1 minute.

Pour the vermouth or white wine into the pan and season to taste with salt and pepper. Return the chicken to the pan. Bring to the boil, reduce the heat to low and simmer for about 20 minutes, or until tender.3 In another large frying pan, heat the butter and add the sliced porcini or wild mushrooms. Stir-fry for about 5 minutes, or until the mushrooms are golden and tender.

Add the porcini or wild mushrooms and any juices to the chicken. Season to taste, then add the chopped oregano. Stir together gently and cook for 1 minute longer. Transfer to a large serving plate and garnish with sprigs of fresh basil, if desired. Serve immediately with rice.

Try this: FOR STARTERS: 42   FOR PUDDING: 360

Crispy Chicken Noodles

SERVES 4

1 medium egg white
2 tsp cornflour
salt and freshly ground
    white pepper
225 g/8 oz boneless
    and skinless chicken
    breast, diced

225 g/8 oz medium
    Chinese egg noodles
200 ml/7 fl oz
    groundnut oil
2 tbsp Chinese
    rice wine
2 tbsp oyster sauce

1 tbsp light soy sauce
300 ml/½ pint chicken stock
1 tbsp cornflour

To garnish:
spring onion curls
toasted cashew nuts

Mix the egg white with the cornflour in a bowl, season to taste with salt and pepper, then add the chicken and stir to coat. Chill in the refrigerator for 20 minutes. Blanch the noodles for 2 minutes in a large saucepan of boiling salted water and drain.

Heat a wok or large frying pan and add 2 tablespoons of the groundnut oil. When hot, spread the noodles evenly over the surface, reduce the heat to low and cook for about 5 minutes, or until browned on one side. Gently turn over, adding extra oil if necessary, and cook until both sides are browned. Reserve and keep warm.

Drain the chicken. Wipe the wok clean, reheat and add the remaining groundnut oil. When hot, add the chicken and stir-fry for 2 minutes. Using a slotted spoon, remove and drain on absorbent kitchen paper. Keep warm.

Wipe the wok clean, reheat and pour in the Chinese rice wine, oyster sauce, soy sauce and chicken stock and season lightly. Bring to the boil. Blend the cornflour to a paste with 2 tablespoons of water and stir into the wok. Cook, stirring, until the sauce has thickened. Cook for a further 1 minute.

Tip the noodles on to warmed plates, top with the crispy chicken pieces and drizzle over the sauce. Garnish with spring onion curls and sprinkle with toasted cashew nuts. Serve immediately.

Try this: FOR STARTERS: 36   FOR PUDDING: 368

Herb–baked Chicken with Tagliatelle

SERVES 4

75 g/3 oz fresh
  white breadcrumbs
3 tbsp olive oil
1 tsp dried oregano
2 tbsp sun-dried
  tomato paste

salt and freshly ground
  black pepper
4 boneless and skinless
  chicken breasts, each
  about 150 g/5 oz
2 x 400 g cans

plum tomatoes
4 tbsp freshly chopped basil
2 tbsp dry white wine
350 g/12 oz tagliatelle
fresh basil sprigs,
  to garnish

Preheat the oven to 200°C/400°F/Gas Mark 6, 15 minute before cooking. Mix together the breadcrumbs, 1 tablespoon of the olive oil, the oregano and tomato paste. Season to taste with salt and pepper. Place the chicken breasts well apart in a roasting tin and coat with the breadcrumb mixture.

Mix the plum tomatoes with the chopped basil and white wine. Season to taste, then spoon evenly round the chicken.

Drizzle the remaining olive oil over the chicken breasts and cook in the preheated oven for 20–30 minutes, or until the chicken is golden and the juices run clear when a skewer is inserted into the flesh.

Meanwhile, bring a large pan of lightly salted water to a rolling boil. Add the pasta and cook according to the packet instructions, or until 'al dente'.

Drain the pasta thoroughly and transfer to warmed serving plates. Arrange the chicken breasts on top of the pasta and spoon over the sauce. Garnish with sprigs of basil and serve immediately.

Try this: FOR STARTERS: 52 FOR PUDDING: 356

Parma Ham–wrapped Chicken with Ribbon Pasta

SERVES 4

4 boneless and skinless
    chicken breasts
salt and freshly ground
    black pepper
12 slices Parma ham
2 tbsp olive oil
350 g/12 oz ribbon pasta

1 garlic clove, peeled and
    chopped
1 bunch spring onions,
    trimmed and
    diagonally sliced
400 g can chopped tomatoes
juice of 1 lemon

150 ml/¼ pint crème fraîche
3 tbsp freshly
    chopped parsley
pinch of sugar
freshly grated
    Parmesan cheese,
    to garnish

Cut each chicken breast into three pieces and season well with salt and pepper. Wrap each chicken piece in a slice of Parma ham to enclose completely, securing if necessary with either fine twine or cocktail sticks.

Heat the oil in a large frying pan and cook the chicken, turning occasionally, for 12–15 minutes, or until thoroughly cooked. Remove from the pan with a slotted spoon and reserve.

Meanwhile, bring a large pan of lightly salted water to a rolling boil. Add the pasta and cook according to the packet instructions, or until 'al dente'.

Add the garlic and spring onions to the frying pan and cook, stirring occasionally, for 2 minutes, or until softened. Stir in the tomatoes, lemon juice and crème fraîche. Bring to the boil, lower the heat and simmer, covered, for 3 minutes. Stir in the parsley and sugar, season to taste, then return the chicken to the pan and heat for 2–3 minutes, or until piping hot.

Drain the pasta thoroughly and mix in the chopped parsley, then spoon on to a warmed serving dish or individual plates. Arrange the chicken and sauce over the pasta. Garnish and serve immediately.

Szechuan Sesame Chicken

SERVES 4

1 medium egg white	1 tbsp sesame seeds	1 tsp whole Szechuan
pinch of salt	2 tsp dark soy sauce	peppercorns, roasted
2 tsp cornflour	2 tsp cider vinegar	2 tbsp spring onion,
450 g/1 lb boneless, skinless	2 tsp chilli bean sauce	trimmed and
chicken breast, cut into	2 tsp sesame oil	finely chopped
7.5 cm/3 inch strips	2 tsp sugar	mixed salad, to serve
300 ml/½ pint groundnut oil	1 tbsp Chinese rice wine	

Beat the egg white with a pinch of salt and the cornflour, pour into a shallow dish and add the chicken strips. Turn to coat, cover with clingfilm and leave in the refrigerator for 20 minutes.

Heat a wok, add the groundnut oil and when hot, add the chicken pieces and stir-fry for 2 minutes or until the chicken turns white. Using a slotted spoon, remove the chicken and drain on absorben kitchen paper. Pour off the oil and reserve 1 tablespoon of the oil. Wipe the wok clean.

Reheat the wok, add 1 tablespoon of the groundnut oil with the sesame seeds and stir-fry for 30 seconds, or until golden. Stir in the dark soy sauce, cider vinegar, chilli bean sauce, sesame oil, sugar, Chinese rice wine, Szechuan peppercorns and the spring onions. Bring to the boil.

Return the chicken to the wok and stir-fry for 2 minutes, making sure that the chicken is coated evenly with the sauce and sesame seeds. Turn into a warmed serving dish and serve immediately with a mixed salad.

Creamy Chicken Stroganoff

SERVES 4

450 g/1 lb skinless chicken
  breast fillets
4 tbsp dry sherry
15 g/½ oz dried
  porcini mushrooms
2 tbsp sunflower oil
25 g/1 oz unsalted butter
1 onion, peeled and sliced

225 g/8 oz chestnut
  mushrooms, wiped
  and sliced
1 tbsp paprika
1 tsp freshly chopped thyme
125 ml/4 fl oz chicken stock
150 ml/¼ pint crème fraîche
salt and freshly ground

black pepper
sprigs of fresh thyme,
  to garnish

To serve:
crème fraîche
freshly cooked rice
  or egg noodles

Cut the chicken into finger-length strips and reserve. Gently warm the sherry in a small saucepan and remove from the heat. Add the porcini mushrooms and leave to soak while preparing the rest of the stir-fry.

Heat a wok, add 1½ tablespoons of the oil and when hot, add the chicken and stir-fry over a high heat for 3–4 minutes, or until lightly browned. Remove from the wok and reserve.

Heat the remaining oil and butter in the wok and gently cook the onion for 5 minutes. Add the chestnut mushrooms and stir-fry for a further 5 minutes, or until tender. Sprinkle in the paprika and thyme and cook for 30 seconds.

Add the porcini mushrooms with their soaking liquid, then stir in the stock and return the chicken to the wok. Cook for 1–2 minutes, or until the chicken is cooked through and tender.

Stir in the crème fraîche and heat until piping hot. Season to taste with salt and pepper. Garnish with sprigs of fresh thyme and serve immediately with a spoonful of crème fraîche and rice or egg noodles.

Try this: FOR STARTERS: 56   FOR PUDDING: 354

Garlic Mushrooms with
Crispy Bacon & Chicken Liver Sauté

SERVES 4

4 large field mushrooms
40 g/1½ oz butter,
  melted and cooled
2 garlic cloves, peeled
  and crushed
1 tbsp sunflower oil
3 rashers smoked streaky

bacon, derinded
  and chopped
4 shallots, peeled and
  thinly sliced
450 g/1 lb chicken livers,
  halved
2 tbsp marsala or

sweet sherry
4 tbsp chicken or
  vegetable stock
6 tbsp double cream
2 tsp freshly chopped thyme
salt and freshly ground
  black pepper

Remove the stalks from the mushrooms and roughly chop. Mix together 25 g/1 oz of the butter and garlic and brush over both sides of the mushroom caps. Place on the rack of a grill pan.

Heat a wok, add the oil and when hot, add the bacon and stir-fry for 2–3 minutes, or until crispy. Remove and reserve. Add the remaining butter to the wok and stir-fry the shallots and chopped mushroom stalks for 4–5 minutes until they are softened.

Add the chicken livers and cook for 3–4 minutes, or until well browned on the outside, but still pink and tender inside. Pour in the marsala or sherry and the stock. Simmer for 1 minute, then stir in the cream, thyme, salt and pepper and half the bacon. Cook for about 30 seconds to heat through.

While the livers are frying, cook the mushroom caps under a hot grill for 3–4 minutes each side, until tender.

Place the mushrooms on warmed serving plates, allowing 1 per person. Spoon the chicken livers over and around the mushrooms. Scatter with the remaining bacon and serve immediately.

Try this: FOR STARTERS: 36   FOR PUDDING: 372

Sesame–coated Turkey with Mango Tabbouleh

SERVES 4

3 turkey breast fillets,
   about 450 g/1 lb, skinned
4 tbsp plain flour
4 tbsp sesame seeds
salt and freshly ground
   black pepper
1 medium egg, lightly beaten
2 tbsp sunflower oil

For the mango tabbouleh:
175 g/6 oz bulgar wheat
2 tbsp olive oil
juice of ½ lemon
6 spring onions,
   trimmed and
   finely chopped
1 red chilli, deseeded

and finely chopped
1 ripe mango, peeled,
   pitted and diced
3 tbsp freshly
   chopped coriander
1 tbsp freshly chopped
   mint leaves

Cut the turkey across the grain into strips. Mix together the flour, sesame seeds, salt and pepper. Dip the turkey strips in the beaten egg, then in the sesame seed mixture to coat. Chill in the refrigerator until ready to cook.

For the tabbouleh, put the bulgar wheat in a large bowl and pour over plenty of boiling water. Cover the bowl with a plate and leave to soak for 20 minutes.

Whisk together the olive oil and lemon juice in a large bowl. Stir in the spring onions, chilli, mango, coriander and mint. Drain the bulgar and squeeze out any excess moisture with your hands, then add to the bowl, season to taste with salt and pepper and mix well.

Heat a wok, add the oil and, when hot, stir-fry the sesame-coated turkey strips in two batches for 4–5 minutes, or until golden, crispy and cooked through. Divide the turkey strips between individual serving plates and serve immediately with the tabbouleh.

Duck in Black Bean Sauce

SERVES 4

450 g/1 lb duck breast,
  skinned
1 tbsp light soy sauce
1 tbsp Chinese rice wine
  or dry sherry
2.5 cm/1 inch piece

fresh root ginger
3 garlic cloves
2 spring onions
2 tbsp Chinese preserved
  black beans
1 tbsp groundnut or

vegetable oil
150 ml/¼ pint chicken stock
shredded spring onions,
  to garnish
freshly cooked noodles,
  to serve

Using a sharp knife, trim the duck breasts, removing any fat. Slice thickly and place in a shallow dish. Mix together the soy sauce and Chinese rice wine or sherry and pour over the duck. Leave to marinate for 1 hour in the refrigerator, then drain and discard the marinade.

Peel the ginger and chop finely. Peel the garlic cloves and either chop finely or crush. Trim the root from the spring onions, discard the outer leaves and chop. Finely chop the black beans.

Heat a wok or large frying pan, add the oil and when very hot, add the ginger, garlic, spring onions and black beans and stir-fry for 30 seconds. Add the drained duck and stir-fry for 3–5 minutes or until the duck is browned.

Add the chicken stock to the wok, bring to the boil, then reduce the heat and simmer for 5 minutes, or until the duck is cooked and the sauce is reduced and thickened. Remove from the heat. Tip on to a bed of freshly cooked noodles, garnish with spring onion shreds and serve immediately.

Try this: FOR STARTERS: 62   FOR PUDDING: 374

Hoisin Duck
& Greens Stir Fry

SERVES 4

350 g/12 oz duck breasts,
  skinned and cut into strips
1 medium egg white, beaten
½ tsp salt
1 tsp sesame oil
2 tsp cornflour
2 tbsp groundnut oil

2 tbsp freshly grated
  root ginger
50 g/2 oz bamboo shoots
50 g/2 oz fine green beans,
  trimmed
50 g/2 oz pak choi, trimmed
2 tbsp hoisin sauce

1 tsp Chinese rice wine
  or dry sherry
zest and juice of ½ orange
strips of orange zest,
  to garnish
freshly steamed egg
  noodles, to serve

Place the duck strips in a shallow dish, then add the egg white, salt, sesame oil and cornflour.
Stir lightly until the duck is coated in the mixture. Cover and chill in the refrigerator for 20 minutes.

Heat the wok until very hot and add the oil. Remove the wok from the heat and add the duck,
stirring continuously to prevent the duck from sticking to the wok. Add the ginger and stir-fry
for 2 minutes. Add the bamboo shoots, the green beans and the pak choi, and stir-fry for
1–2 minutes until wilted.

Mix together the hoisin sauce, the Chinese rice wine or sherry and the orange zest and juice.
Pour into the wok and stir to coat the duck and vegetables. Stir-fry for 1–2 minutes, or until
the duck and vegetables are tender. Garnish with the strips of orange zest and serve
immediately with freshly steamed egg noodles.

Honey–glazed Duck in Kumquat Sauce

SERVES 4

4 duck breast fillets
1 tbsp light soy sauce
1 tsp sesame oil
1 tbsp clear honey
3 tbsp brandy
1 tbsp sunflower oil

2 tbsp caster sugar
1 tbsp white wine vinegar
150 ml/¼ pint orange juice
125 g/4 oz kumquats,
   thinly sliced
2 tsp cornflour

salt and freshly ground
   black pepper
fresh watercress,
   to garnish
basmati and wild rice,
   to serve

Thinly slice the duck breasts and put in a shallow bowl. Mix together the soy sauce, sesame oil, honey and 1 tablespoon of brandy. Pour over the duck, stir well, cover and marinate in the refrigerator for at least 1 hour.

Heat a wok until hot, add the sunflower oil and swirl it round to coat the sides. Drain the duck, reserving the marinade, and stir-fry over a high heat for 2–3 minutes, or until browned. Remove from the wok; reserve.

Wipe the wok clean with absorbent kitchen paper. Add the sugar, vinegar and 1 tablespoon of water. Gently heat until the sugar dissolves, then boil until a rich golden colour. Pour in the orange juice, then the remaining brandy. Stir in the kumquat slices and simmer for 5 minutes.

Blend the cornflour with 1 tablespoon of cold water. Add to the wok and simmer for 2–3 minutes, stirring until thickened. Return the duck to the wok and cook gently for 1–2 minutes, or until warmed through. Season to taste with salt and pepper. Spoon onto warmed plates and garnish with fresh watercress leaves. Serve immediately with freshly cooked basmati and wild rice.

Try this: FOR STARTERS: 42   FOR PUDDING: 362

Stir–fried Greens

SERVES 4

450 g/1 lb Chinese leaves
225 g/8 oz pak choi
225 g/8 oz broccoli florets
1 tbsp sesame seeds
1 tbsp groundnut oil
1 tbsp fresh root ginger,
   peeled and finely chopped

3 garlic cloves, peeled
   and finely chopped
2 red chillies, deseeded
   and split in half
50 ml/2 fl oz chicken stock
2 tbsp Chinese rice wine
1 tbsp dark soy sauce

1 tsp light soy sauce
2 tsp black bean sauce
freshly ground black pepper
2 tsp sugar
1 tsp sesame oil

Separate the Chinese leaves and pak choi and wash well. Cut into 2.5 cm/1 inch strips. Separate the broccoli into small florets. Heat a wok or large frying pan, add the sesame seeds and stir-fry for 30 seconds or until browned.

Add the oil to the wok and when hot, add the ginger, garlic and chillies and stir-fry for 30 seconds. Add the broccoli and stir-fry for 1 minute. Add the Chinese leaves and pak choi and stir-fry for a further 1 minute.

Pour the chicken stock and Chinese rice wine into the wok with the soy and black bean sauces. Season to taste with pepper and add the sugar. Reduce the heat and simmer for 6–8 minutes, or until the vegetables are tender but still firm to the bite. Tip into a warmed serving dish, removing the chillies if preferred. Drizzle with the sesame oil and serve immediately.

Vegetables in Coconut Milk with Rice Noodles

SERVES 4

75 g/3 oz creamed coconut
1 tsp salt
2 tbsp sunflower oil
2 garlic cloves, peeled and
    finely chopped
2 red peppers, deseeded
    and cut into thin strips
2.5 cm/1 inch piece of fresh
    root ginger, peeled and
    cut into thin strips
125 g/4 oz baby sweetcorn
2 tsp cornflour
2 medium ripe but still
    firm avocados
1 small Cos lettuce,
    cut into thick strips
freshly cooked rice noodles,
    to serve

Roughly chop the creamed coconut, place in a bowl with the salt, then pour over 600 ml/1 pint of boiling water. Stir until the coconut has dissolved completely and reserve.

Heat a wok or large frying pan, add the oil and when hot, add the chopped garlic, sliced peppers and ginger. Cook for 30 seconds, then cover and cook very gently for 10 minutes or until the peppers are soft.

Pour in the reserved coconut milk and bring to the boil. Stir in the baby sweetcorn, cover and simmer for 5 minutes. Blend the cornflour with 2 teaspoons of water, pour into the wok and cook, stirring, for 2 minutes or until thickened slightly.

Cut the avocados in half, peel, remove the stone and slice. Add to the wok with the lettuce strips and stir until well mixed and heated through. Serve immediately on a bed of rice noodles.

Try this: FOR STARTERS: 26   FOR PUDDING: 368

Tomato & Courgette Herb Tart

SERVES 4

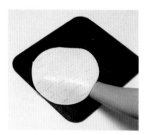

4 tbsp olive oil	pastry, thawed if frozen	175 g/6 oz rindless fresh
1 onion, peeled and	1 small egg, beaten	soft goats' cheese
finely chopped	2 tbsp freshly	4 ripe plum tomatoes, sliced
3 garlic cloves, peeled	chopped rosemary	1 medium courgette,
and crushed	2 tbsp freshly	trimmed and sliced
400 g/14 oz prepared puff	chopped parsley	thyme sprigs, to garnish

Preheat the oven to 230°C/450°F/Gas Mark 8. Heat 2 tablespoons of the oil in a large frying pan. Fry the onion and garlic for about 4 minutes until softened and reserve.

Roll out the pastry on a lightly floured surface, and cut out a 30.5 cm/12 inch circle. Brush the pastry with a little beaten egg, then prick all over with a fork. Transfer on to a dampened baking sheet and bake in the preheated oven for 10 minutes.

Turn the pastry over and brush with a little more egg. Bake for 5 more minutes, then remove from the oven.

Mix together the onion, garlic and herbs with the goats' cheese and spread over the pastry. Arrange the tomatoes and courgettes over the goats' cheese and drizzle with the remaining oil.

Bake for 20–25 minutes, or until the pastry is golden brown and the topping bubbling. Garnish with the thyme sprigs and serve immediately.

Puddings & Desserts

Creamy Puddings with Mixed Berry Compote

SERVES 6

300 ml/½ pint half-fat
   double cream
1 x 250 g carton
   ricotta cheese

50 g/2 oz caster sugar
125 g/4 oz white chocolate,
   broken into pieces
350 g/12 oz mixed summer

fruits such as
   strawberries, blueberries
   and raspberries
2 tbsp Cointreau

Set the freezer to rapid freeze. Whip the cream until soft peaks form. Fold in the ricotta cheese and half the sugar.

Place the chocolate in a bowl set over a saucepan of simmering water. Stir until melted.

Remove from the heat and leave to cool, stirring occasionally. Stir into the cheese mixture until well blended.

Spoon the mixture into six individual pudding moulds and level the surface of each pudding with the back of a spoon. Place in the freezer and freeze for 4 hours.

Place the fruits and the remaining sugar in a pan and heat gently, stirring occasionally until the sugar has dissolved and the juices are just beginning to run. Stir in the Cointreau to taste.

Dip the pudding moulds in hot water for 30 seconds and invert on to six serving plates. Spoon the fruit compote over the puddings and serve immediately. Remember to return the freezer to its normal setting.

Try this: FOR STARTERS: 54   FOR MAIN MEAL: 200

Lemon Surprise

SERVES 4

75 g /3 oz margarine
175 g/6 oz caster sugar
3 medium eggs, separated
75 g/3 oz self-raising flour

450 ml/¾ pint
 semi-skimmed milk
juice of 2 lemons
juice of 1 orange

2 tsp icing sugar
lemon twists, to decorate
sliced strawberries,
 to serve

Preheat the oven to 190°C/375°F/Gas Mark 5. Lightly oil a deep ovenproof dish.

Beat together the margarine and sugar until pale and fluffy. Add the egg yolks, one at a time, with 1 tablespoon of the flour and beat well after each addition. Once added, stir in the remaining flour.

Stir in the milk, 4 tablespoons of the lemon juice and 3 tablespoons of the orange juice. Whis the egg whites until stiff and fold into the pudding mixture with a metal spoon or rubber spatula until well combined. Pour into the prepared dish.

Stand the dish in a roasting tin and pour in just enough boiling water to come halfway up the sides of the dish.

Bake in the preheated oven for 45 minutes, until well risen and spongy to the touch.

Remove the pudding from the oven and sprinkle with the icing sugar. Decorate with the lemon twists and serve immediately with the strawberries.

Coffee & Peach Creams

SERVES 4

4 peaches
50 g/2 oz caster sugar
2 tbsp coffee
 essence

200 g carton Greek yogurt
300 g carton ready-
 made custard

To decorate:
peach slices
sprigs of mint
crème fraîche

Cut the peaches in half and remove the stones. Place the peaches in a large bowl,
cover with boiling water and leave for 2–3 minutes.

Drain the peaches, then carefully remove the skin. Using a sharp knife, halve the peaches.

Place the caster sugar in a saucepan and add 50 ml/2 fl oz water. Bring the sugar mixture to
the boil, stirring occasionally, until the sugar has dissolved. Boil rapidly for about 2 minutes.

Add the peaches and coffee essence to the pan. Remove from the heat and allow the peach
mixture to cool.

Meanwhile mix together the Greek yogurt and custard until well combined.

Divide the peaches between the four glass dishes. Spoon over the custard mixture then top
with remaining peach mixture.

Chill for 30 minutes and then serve, decorated with peach slices, mint sprigs and a little
crème fraîche.

Try this: FOR STARTERS: 24 FOR MAIN MEAL: 106

Chocolate Mousse

SERVES 6

175 g/6 oz milk or plain
   chocolate orange
535 g carton ready-
   made custard

450 ml/¾ pint
   double cream
12 Cape gooseberries,
   to decorate

sweet biscuits,
   to serve

Break the chocolate into segments and place in a bowl set over a saucepan of simmering water. Leave until melted, stirring occasionally. Remove the bowl in the pan from the heat and allow the melted chocolate to cool slightly.

Place the custard in a bowl and fold the melted chocolate into it using a metal spoon or rubber spatula. Stir well until completely combined.

Pour the cream into a small bowl and whip until the cream forms soft peaks. Using a metal spoon or rubber spatula fold in most of the whipped cream into the chocolate mixture.

Spoon into six tall glasses and carefully top with the remaining cream.

Leave the desserts to chill in the refrigerator for at least 1 hour or preferably overnight.

Peel back the skins from the gooseberries to form petal shapes and use to decorate the chocolate desserts. Serve with the sweet biscuits.

Crunchy Rhubarb Crumble

SERVES 6

125 g/4 oz plain flour	50 g/2 oz demerara sugar	450 g/1 lb fresh rhubarb
50 g/2 oz softened butter	1 tbsp sesame seeds	50 g/2 oz caster sugar
50 g/2 oz rolled oats	½ tsp ground cinnamon	custard or cream, to serve

Preheat the oven to 180°C/350°F/Gas Mark 4. Place the flour in a large bowl and cut the butter into cubes. Add to the flour and rub in with the fingertips until the mixture looks like fine breadcrumbs, or blend for a few seconds in a food processor.

Stir in the rolled oats, demerara sugar, sesame seeds and cinnamon. Mix well and reserve.

Prepare the rhubarb by removing the thick ends of the stalks and cut diagonally into 2.5 cm/1 inch chunks. Wash thoroughly and pat dry with a clean tea towel. Place the rhubarb in a 1.1 litre/2 pint pie dish.

Sprinkle the caster sugar over the rhubarb and top with the reserved crumble mixture. Level the top of the crumble so that all the fruit is well covered and press down firmly. If liked, sprinkle the top with a little extra caster sugar.

Place on a baking sheet and bake in the preheated oven for 40–50 minutes, or until the fruit is soft and the topping is golden brown. Sprinkle the pudding with some more caster sugar and serve hot with custard or cream.

Crème Brûlée with Sugared Raspberries

SERVES 6

600 ml/1 pint fresh
   whipping cream
4 medium egg yolks

75 g/3 oz caster sugar
½ tsp vanilla essence
25 g/1 oz demerara sugar

175 g/6 oz fresh raspberries

Preheat the oven to 150°C/300°F/Gas Mark 2. Pour the cream into a bowl and place over a saucepan of gently simmering water. Heat gently but do not allow to boil.

Meanwhile, whisk together the egg yolks, 50 g/2 oz of the caster sugar and the vanilla essence. When the cream is warm, pour it over the egg mixture briskly whisking until it is mixed completely. Pour into 6 individual ramekin dishes and place in a roasting tin.

Fill the tin with sufficient water to come halfway up the sides of the dishes. Bake in the preheated oven for about 1 hour, or until the puddings are set. To test if set, carefully insert a round bladed knife into the centre, if the knife comes out clean they are set.

Remove the puddings from the roasting tin and allow to cool. Chill in the refrigerator, preferably overnight.

Sprinkle the sugar over the top of each dish and place the puddings under a preheated hot grill.

When the sugar has caramelised and turned deep brown, remove from the heat and cool. Chill the puddings in the refrigerator for 2–3 hours before serving.

Toss the raspberries in the remaining caster sugar and sprinkle over the top of each dish. Serve with a little extra cream if liked.

Try this: FOR STARTERS: 32   FOR MAIN MEAL: 120

Chocolate Sponge Pudding with Fudge Sauce

SERVES 4

75 g/3 oz butter
75 g/3 oz caster sugar
50 g/2 oz plain dark
   chocolate, melted
50 g/2 oz self-raising flour
25 g/1 oz drinking chocolate
1 large egg

1 tbsp icing sugar,
   to dust
crème fraîche,
   to serve

For the fudge sauce:
50 g/2 oz soft light

brown sugar
1 tbsp cocoa powder
40 g/1½ oz pecan nuts,
   roughly chopped
25 g/1 oz caster sugar
300 ml/½ pint hot,
   strong black coffee

Preheat the oven to 170°C/325°F/Gas Mark 3. Oil a 900 ml/1½ pint pie dish.

Cream the butter and the sugar together in a large bowl until light and fluffy. Stir in the melted chocolate, flour, drinking chocolate and egg and mix together. Turn the mixture into the prepared dish and level the surface.

To make the fudge sauce, blend the brown sugar, cocoa powder and pecan nuts together and sprinkle evenly over the top of the pudding.

Stir the caster sugar into the hot black coffee until it has dissolved. Carefully pour the coffee over the top of the pudding.

Bake in the preheated oven for 50–60 minutes, until the top is firm to touch. There will now be a rich sauce underneath the sponge.

Remove from the oven, dust with icing sugar and serve hot with crème fraîche.

Try this: FOR STARTERS: 60   FOR MAIN MEAL: 110

Golden Castle Pudding

SERVES 4–6

125 g/4 oz butter	vanilla essence	4 tbsp golden syrup
125 g/4 oz caster sugar	2 medium eggs, beaten	crème fraîche or ready-made
a few drops of	125 g/4 oz self-raising flour	custard, to serve

Preheat the oven to 180°C/350°F/Gas Mark 4. Lightly oil 4–6 individual pudding bowls and place a small circle of lightly oiled non-stick baking or greaseproof paper in the base of each one.

Place the butter and caster sugar in a large bowl, then beat together until the mixture is pale and creamy. Stir in the vanilla essence and gradually add the beaten eggs, a little at a time. Add a tablespoon of flour after each addition of egg and beat well.

When the mixture is smooth, add the remaining flour and fold in gently. Add a tablespoon of water and mix to form a soft mixture that will drop easily off a spoon.

Spoon enough mixture into each basin to come halfway up the tin, allowing enough space for the puddings to rise. Place on a baking sheet and bake in the preheated oven for about 25 minutes until firm and golden brown.

Allow the puddings to stand for 5 minutes. Discard the paper circle and turn out on to individual serving plates.

Warm the golden syrup in a small saucepan and pour a little over each pudding. Serve hot with the crème fraîche or custard.

Cherry Batter Pudding

SERVES 4

450 g/1 lb fresh cherries (or
   425 g can pitted cherries)
50 g/2 oz plain flour
pinch of salt

3 tbsp caster sugar
2 medium eggs
300 ml/½ pint milk
40 g/1½ oz butter

1 tbsp rum
extra caster sugar, to dredge
fresh cream, to serve

Preheat the oven to 220°C/425°F/Gas Mark 7. Lightly oil a 900 ml/1½ pint shallow baking dish.

Rinse the cherries, drain well and remove the stones (using a cherry stoner if possible).
If using canned cherries, drain well, discard the juice and place in the prepared dish.

Sift the flour and salt into a large bowl. Stir in 2 tablespoons of the caster sugar and make
a well in the centre. Beat the eggs, then pour into the well of the dry ingredients.

Warm the milk and slowly pour into the well, beating throughout and gradually
drawing in the flour from the sides of the bowl. Continue until a smooth batter has formed.

Melt the butter in a small saucepan over a low heat, then stir into the batter with the rum.
Reserve for 15 minutes, then beat again until smooth and easy to pour.

Pour into the prepared baking dish and bake in the preheated oven for 30–35 minutes,
or until golden brown and set.

Remove the pudding from the oven, sprinkle with the remaining sugar and serve hot with
plenty of fresh cream.

Vanilla & Lemon Panna Cotta with Raspberry Sauce

SERVES 6

900 ml/1½ pints
  double cream
1 vanilla pod, split
100 g/3½ oz caster sugar

zest of 1 lemon
3 sheets gelatine
5 tbsp milk
450 g/1 lb raspberries

3–4 tbsp icing sugar, to taste
1 tbsp lemon juice
extra lemon zest,
  to decorate

Put the cream, vanilla pod and sugar into a saucepan. Bring to the boil, then simmer for 10 minutes until slightly reduced, stirring to prevent scalding. Remove from the heat, stir in the lemon zest and remove the vanilla pod.

Soak the gelatine in the milk for 5 minutes, or until softened. Squeeze out any excess milk and add to the hot cream. Stir well until dissolved.

Pour the cream mixture into six ramekins or mini pudding moulds and leave in the refrigerator for 4 hours, or until set.

Meanwhile, put 175 g/6 oz of the raspberries in a food processor with the icing sugar and lemon juice. Blend to a purée then pass the mixture through a sieve. Fold in the remaining raspberries with a metal spoon or rubber spatula and chill in the refrigerator until ready to serve.

To serve, dip each of the moulds into hot water for a few seconds, then turn out on to six individual serving plates. Spoon some of the raspberry sauce over and around the panna cotta, decorate with extra lemon zest and serve.

Ricotta Cheesecake with Strawberry Coulis

SERVES 6-8

125 g/4 oz digestive biscuits
100 g/3½ oz candied
   peel, chopped
65 g/2½ oz butter, melted
150 ml/¼ pint crème fraîche

575 g/4 oz ricotta cheese
100 g/3½ oz caster sugar
1 vanilla pod, seeds only
2 large eggs
225 g/8 oz strawberries

25–50 g/1–2 oz caster sugar,
   to taste
zest and juice of 1 orange

Preheat the oven to 170˚C/325˚F/Gas Mark 3. Line a 20.5 cm/8 inch springform tin with baking parchment. Place the biscuits into a food processor together with the peel. Blend until the biscuits are crushed and the peel is chopped. Add 50 g/2 oz of the melted butter and process until mixed. Tip into the tin and spread evenly over the bottom. Press firmly into place and reserve.

Blend together the crème fraîche, ricotta cheese, sugar, vanilla seeds and eggs in a food processor. With the motor running, add the remaining melted butter and blend for a few seconds. Pour the mixture on to the base. Transfer to the preheated oven and cook for about 1 hour, until set and risen round the edges, but slightly wobbly in the centre. Switch off the oven and allow to cool there. chill in the refrigerator for at least 8 hours, or preferably overnight.

Wash and drain the strawberries. Hull the fruit and remove any soft spots. Put into the food processor along with 25 g/1 oz of the sugar and orange juice and zest. Blend until smooth. Add the remaining sugar to taste. Pass through a sieve to remove seeds and chill in the refrigerator until needed.

Cut the cheesecake into wedges, spoon over some of the strawberry coulis and serve.

Summer Fruit Semifreddo

SERVES 6–8

225 g/8 oz raspberries
125 g/4 oz blueberries
125 g/4 oz redcurrants
50 g/2 oz icing sugar

juice of 1 lemon
1 vanilla pod, split
50 g/2 oz sugar
4 large eggs, separated

600 ml/1 pint double cream
pinch of salt
fresh redcurrants,
    to decorate

Wash and hull or remove stalks from the fruits, as necessary, then put them into a food processor or blender with the icing sugar and lemon juice. Blend to a purée, pour into a jug and chill in the refrigerator, until needed.

Remove the seeds from the vanilla pod by opening the pod and scraping with the back of a knife. Add the seeds to the sugar and whisk with the egg yolks until pale and thick.

In another bowl, whip the cream until soft peaks form. Do not overwhip. In a third bowl, whip the egg whites with the salt until stiff peaks form.

Using a large metal spoon – to avoid knocking any air from the mixture – fold together the fruit purée, egg yolk mixture, the cream and egg whites. Transfer the mixture to a round, shallow, lidded freezer box and put into the freezer until almost frozen. If the mixture freezes solid, thaw in the refrigerator until semi-frozen. Turn out the semi-frozen mixture, cut into wedges and serve decorated with a few fresh redcurrants. If the mixture thaws completely, eat immediately and do not refreeze.

Try this: FOR STARTERS: 62   FOR MAIN MEAL: 168

Baked Stuffed Amaretti Peaches

SERVES 4

4 ripe peaches
grated zest and juice
  of 1 lemon
75 g/3 oz Amaretti biscuits
50 g/2 oz chopped blanched

almonds, toasted
50 g/2 oz pine nuts, toasted
40 g/1½ oz light
  muscovado sugar
50 g/2 oz butter

1 medium egg yolk
2 tsp clear honey
crème fraîche or Greek
  yogurt, to serve

Preheat the oven to 180°C/350°F/Gas Mark 4. Halve the peaches and remove the stones. Take a very thin slice from the bottom of each peach half so that it will sit flat on the baking sheet. Dip the peach halves in lemon juice and arrange on a baking sheet.

Crush the Amaretti biscuits lightly and put into a large bowl. Add the almonds, pine nuts, sugar, lemon zest and butter. Work with the fingertips until the mixture resembles coarse breadcrumbs. Add the egg yolk and mix well until the mixture is just binding.

Divide the Amaretti and nut mixture between the peach halves, pressing down lightly. Bake in the preheated oven for 15 minutes, or until the peaches are tender and the filling is golden. Remove from the oven and drizzle with the honey.

Place two peach halves on each serving plate and spoon over a little crème fraîche or Greek yogurt, then serve.

Zabaglione with Rum–soaked Raisin Compote

SERVES 6

2 tbsp raisins
1 strip thinly pared
   lemon zest
½ tsp ground cinnamon

3 tbsp Marsala wine
3 medium egg yolks
3 tbsp caster sugar
125 ml/4 fl oz dry white wine

150 ml/¼ pint double cream,
   lightly whipped
crisp biscuits,
   to serve

Put the raisins in a small bowl with the lemon zest and ground cinnamon. Pour over the Marsala wine to cover and leave to macerate for at least one hour. When the raisins are plump, lift out of the Marsala wine and reserve the raisins and wine, discarding the lemon zest.

In a large heatproof bowl, mix together the egg yolks and sugar. Add the white wine and Marsala wine and stir well to combine. Put the bowl over a saucepan of simmering water, ensuring that the bottom of the bowl does not touch the water. Whisk constantly until the mixture doubles in bulk.

Remove from the heat and continue whisking for about 5 minutes until the mixture has cooled slightly. Fold in the raisins and then immediately fold in the whipped cream. Spoon into dessert glasses or goblets and serve with crisp biscuits.

Try this: FOR STARTERS: 48   FOR MAIN MEAL: 136

Tiramisu

SERVES 4

225 g/8 oz mascarpone
cheese
25 g/1 oz icing sugar, sifted
150 ml/¼ pint strong brewed
coffee, chilled

300 ml/½ pint double cream
3 tbsp coffee liqueur
125 g/4 oz Savoiardi or
sponge finger biscuits
50 g/2 oz plain dark

chocolate, grated or
made into small curls
cocoa powder, for dusting
assorted summer berries,
to serve

Lightly oil and line a 900 g/2 lb loaf tin with a piece of clingfilm. Put the mascarpone cheese and icing sugar into a large bowl and using a rubber spatula, beat until smooth. Stir in 2 tablespoons of chilled coffee and mix thoroughly.

Whip the cream with 1 tablespoon of the coffee liqueur until just thickened. Stir a spoonful of the whipped cream into the mascarpone mixture, then fold in the rest. Spoon half of the the mascarpone mixture into the prepared loaf tin and smooth the top.

Put the remaining coffee and coffee liqueur into a shallow dish just bigger than the biscuits. Using half of the biscuits, dip one side of each biscuit into the coffee mixture, then arrange on top of the mascarpone mixture in a single layer. Spoon the rest of the mascarpone mixture over the biscuits and smooth the top.

Dip the remaining biscuits in the coffee mixture and arrange on top of the mascarpone mixture. Drizzle with any remaining coffee mixture. Cover with clingfilm and chill in the refrigerator for 4 hours.

Carefully turn the tiramisu out on to a large serving plate and sprinkle with the grated chocolate or chocolate curls. Dust with cocoa powder, cut into slices and serve with a few summer berries.

Stir–fried Bananas & Peaches with Rum Butterscotch Sauce

SERVES 4

2 medium-firm bananas
1 tbsp caster sugar
2 tsp lime juice
4 firm, ripe peaches
   or nectarines

1 tbsp sunflower oil

For the rum
   butterscotch sauce:
50 g/2 oz unsalted butter

50 g/2 oz soft light
   brown sugar
125 g/4 oz demerara sugar
300 ml/½ pint double cream
2 tbsp dark rum

Peel the bananas and cut into 2.5 cm/1 inch diagonal slices. Place in a bowl and sprinkle with the caster sugar and lime juice and stir until lightly coated. Reserve.

Place the peaches or nectarines in a large bowl and pour over boiling water to cover. Leave for 30 seconds, then plunge them into cold water and peel off their skins. Cut each one into 8 thick slices, discarding the stone.

Heat a wok, add the oil and swirl it round the wok to coat the sides. Add the fruit and cook for 3–4 minutes, shaking the wok and gently turning the fruit until lightly browned. Spoon the fruit into a warmed serving bowl and clean the wok with absorbent kitchen paper.

Add the butter and sugars to the wok and stir continuously over a very low heat until the sugar has dissolved. Remove from the heat and leave to cool for 2–3 minutes.

Stir the cream and rum into the sugar syrup and return to the heat. Bring to the boil and simmer for 2 minutes, stirring continuously until smooth. Leave for 2–3 minutes to cool slightly, then serve warm with the stir-fried peaches and bananas.

Try this: FOR STARTERS: 44   FOR MAIN MEAL: 160

Index